An
Italian Family
Reunion
Cookbook

An Italian Family Reunion Cookbook

Gail Sforza Brewer

Illustrations by Alice D'Onofrio

St. Martin's Press   New York

Library of Congress Cataloging in Publication Data

Brewer, Gail Sforza.
    An Italian family reunion cookbook.

    1. Cookery, Italian. I. Title.
TX723.B723   641.5945   81-16621
ISBN 0-312-43922-9   AACR2

Design by Mina Greenstein
10 9 8 7 6 5 4 3 2 1
First Edition

ACKNOWLEDGMENTS

THANKS TO all who generously gave of their time to help me with this book, and special thanks to: Charlotte Mayerson, who first encouraged me to work on it; Charlie Gerras, who put me in touch with St. Martin's; Jane Price, who supported the project early on; Les Pockell, my editor, who appreciated the idea right away; Sue Tennenbaum, who assisted with the editing; Tessie Sforza, my aunt, keeper of the family genealogy and the person who interested me in books as a child by loaning me some from her personal library long before the public library would issue me a card; Josephine Tramacera, who arranged interviews with members of the Società Pugliese and took a keen interest in the book despite her own failing health; Beatrice DeSantis of the Society of SS. Cosma and Damiano and Larrie Capozella and Bill DiSchiavo, of St. Anthony's Church, Utica, New York, whose dedication to the feast of the saintly physicians brought back fond memories; Gabe Alessandroni, proprietor of the Florentine Pastry Shop, Utica, New York, for invaluable information and good-humored advice about the fancy desserts; Alice D'Onofrio, the artist, whose lively illustrations emerged after hours and hours of sifting through old family photographs; and Margot Edwards, whose poem, "a woman's life," kept me focused through long hours of reminiscence and rewrites.

My husband, Tom Brewer, M.D., served as chief child-care person for far longer than I'd estimated at the outset, but, of course, there were also some fringe benefits involved for him—he got to participate in the recipe-tasting!

To my family, my deepest affection and gratitude for being there as I was growing up. In ways you will never know, you have given me the personal resources I have to carry me through adult life:

Mother:
   Elsie Jean Hickernell Sforza;
Father:
   Joseph Sforza;
Sisters:
   Camille Sforza Rose;
   Linda Sforza Tooke;
   Beth Anne Sforza;
Aunts and Uncles:
   Michael Sforza † ;
   Rose Penge Sforza † ;
   Josephine Fontana Sforza;
   Esther Sforza Montalbano;
   Fortunato Montalbana
      (Fred);
   Aioley Sforza;
   Helen Story Sforza (Tessie);
   Vito Sforza † ;
   Jane Allenby Sforza † ;
   Antonetta Sforza Winterton
      (Toni);
   Raymond Winterton;
   Anna Sforza Usborne;
   Robert Usborne;
   Mildred Sforza Yeman;
   Donald Yeman;
My Cousins:
   Thomas Montalbano;
   Dennis Montalbano;
   Denise Montalbano;
   Marie Catherine Sforza † ;
   John Sforza;
   Diana Winterton;
   Raymond Arthur Winterton;
Gary Winterton;
Carl Winterton;
Dale Winterton † ;
David Winterton † ;
Michael Usborne;
James Usborne;
Donald Usborne;
John Usborne;
Andrew Usborne;
Robert Usborne;
Beverly Yeman;
Donna Yeman;
My Father's Cousins:
Esther Virgilio Ruggerio;
Genevieve Virgilio
   Garramone † ;
Mamie Virgilio Reed;
Lena Virgilio Tomaino;
Frank Virgilio;
Carlo Virgilio;
Grace Virgilio Evans;
Laura Virgilio Fanelli;
Mary Virgilio Ashcraft;
John Semeraro;
Carlo Semeraro;
Antoinette Semeraro;
Thomas Semararo;
Esther Semeraro † ;
Angie Argento Crescenza;
Mary Argento Granada;
Frank Argento;
Josephine Argento
   Tramacera † .

"What is passed down to us from our fathers, we must learn again in order to make it our own."—Goethe, *Faust*

Croton-on-Hudson, March 8, 1981

CONTENTS

In loving memory of my grandparents

Maria Stella Perrino and Carlo Sforza

(1890–1966)   (1886–1973)

PREFACE

"*T*HERE WAS one event to look forward to that took on a kind of mythic quality . . . the annual picnic at a meadow on the shores of Lake Petulia . . . Umbertina's children and grandchildren gathered together there to celebrate themselves as a family, to meet and eat and pay homage to Umbertina, the old lady in black who sat under a tree and was served food all day and given babies to kiss.

"For Umbertina the picnic was her lifetime spread before her . . . Daughters and daughters-in-law in sleeveless white frocks and white stockings kept coming up in a steady stream with the trays of food they had prepared . . . fried chicken parts, her favorite fried sweet peppers to be eaten in huge chunks of fresh-baked crusty bread, tomatoes sliced and dressed with chopped basil, fresh corn on the cob, eggplant fritters, stuffed zucchini, huge tubs of fresh salad greens, whole forms of caciocavallo cheese.

"In her old age, it was the event that pleased her most, more than Christmas or Easter or any of the saints' days. She lived with the memory of it through the long winters; and by the time spring came and she could go out in her backyard and start the rows of corn, put in the stakes for the beans and tomatoes, and nurse the first tender lettuces and herbs, she would be planting for the coming picnic."

—Helen Barolini, *Umbertina*

Delivering produce
to the Italian specialty store

1

A Family Feast

"*MANGIA! MANGIA!*" Grandma would urge, ladling out the steaming, golden chicken soup with the plump grains of Italian rice. And in all the years we sat at her table, I don't think we ever let her down. We were a family that believed in food.

"We" consisted of my grandmother and grandfather, Maria Stella and Carlo Sforza, their eight children and their spouses, and the 21 grandchildren (of which I was the first-born). We gathered whenever there was something special to commemorate: a baptism, a First Communion, Saints' Days, Christmases, Easters and Thanksgivings, weddings, anniversaries, birthdays and funerals. We gathered when there was nothing special to commemorate, just a desire to spend some time together: the every-Sunday-afternoon dinner at Grandma's farm. And when we gathered, we ate.

By far the most eagerly anticipated of all the year's celebrations rolled a bit of each of the others into one: the day of our family reunion. On this summer day our mothers (and fathers) would prepare all the family's favorite foods and serve them up in one glorious, morning-'til-night extravaganza, a feast in honor of the family itself.

Growing up, we kids anticipated the reunion more than any

other day (with the possible exception of Christmas morning). Today, 30 years later, we're still having the reunion, and now our children look forward to it the same way. Just as the youthful, buoyant enthusiasm remains unchanged, so does the menu—homemade Italian specialties, many from ingredients that still originate right there on the farm, just as in Grandma's day. This book is the first collection of these special recipes for the foods so many Italian people everywhere grew up on, the foods that mean home and family and good times to us even today.

We felt it was necessary to set aside a reunion day once a year because even though we 41 Sforzas saw each other at least once a week the year 'round, we were only a third of the entire family. The other two-thirds were my father's cousins, the Semeraros, the Virgilios and the Argentos. Their mothers had been my grandfather's older sisters and cousin, Grace, Anna and Antonia. They all lived in the city, Utica, New York, about 25 miles from our hundred-acre strawberry farm outside Oneida. While there was a good bit of visiting back and forth (especially in the heat of summer when we country cousins could expect a great rush of company on Sunday afternoon), reunion day brought *all of us* together at once.

What an exuberant, chatty mob! My grandmother and grandfather were the sole surviving representatives of their generation. There were 51 in my father's age group. In mine, 59 (before we started to marry). We filled the house, spilled off the porch out onto the lawn, and packed the long wooden tables set up under a gaily striped tent. And even we children were always admonished to eat lightly for a day or two before the reunion so we'd be in the proper frame of mind to enter into the spirit of the day, that is, to eat as if there would be no tomorrow!

There would often be guests at the reunion, people from the Old Country, then already in their sixties and seventies, who had been spending their Sunday afternoons in the country with my grandparents ever since they all arrived from Italy 40 years before. If they happened to show up (in those days people felt comfortable just dropping by to sit and talk and maybe play some cards on the front lawn or under the breezy shade of the maples—no invitations required), they would be treated like members of the family. In fact, it's not improbable that those old men in black vests and pocket watches and old ladies in black dresses and black stockings *were* some sort of distant relations—cousins of our cousins' cousins, perhaps. Generally, though, they were called *paesano* by my grandfather, signifying that the bond we shared arose from our common origin in the same province of Italy (Apulia, the heel of the boot). And next to blood there was no stronger tie than this.

I spent many afternoons of my childhood stretched out with a book on the front porch glider, half-listening to the languorous babble of Italian from the grownups on the other side of the bushes. My younger sisters and cousins would be racing from one end of the house to the other, chasing each other around the side yard, or dashing off to look at the sheep, the chickens or the mean old goat. Sometimes I, too, joined in. But more often than not I would sit there on the glider, the cadence and rhythm of the familiar yet foreign language breaking over me, ever so gradually coming to an awareness of my place in the far-flung, intricate network of relationships that was our family. A decade later, studying Italian in college, I came upon the proverb, "Tutto il mondo è paese" (All the world is kin), and flushed with the warmth of instant recognition. Others before me had sensed these relationships and expressed them perfectly. I had concluded many years before, on the porch, that there could hardly be anybody in the world who wasn't related to me in one way or another!

From time to time the reunion would be planned for a picnic grove or lakeside hall that catered clambakes, but the favored spot was the farm. For most of us in those days it was the one place we thought of as home. For me, it still is. My mother, a girl from an old Pennsylvania Quaker family, left for her wedding from this house in January of 1944 (there's a wonderful picture of my aunts easing the elaborately decorated wedding cake gingerly down the icy back steps en route to the reception). My parents lived upstairs for the early months of their marriage, making it likely that I was conceived here shortly before they moved to their own small farm a few miles away. And it was to this house that my mother and I were brought to stay with Grandma in the first days after my birth. My mother's own mother had died five years before, so when the time came to learn baby care, she turned to my grandmother, just as she had for lessons in cooking my father's customary Italian foods. Grandma spoke little English and my mother no Italian, but they managed very well. I grew up, and my mother became one of the best cooks in the family.

About the year of the first reunion the road that passes by the front of the farmhouse was paved. Except for that, the farmstead looks much as it did when my grandmother saw it for the first time in the spring of 1930. The white frame house, a typical central New York farmhouse, stands opposite acres of strawberry rows. Beyond are the 20 acres of woods that are also part of the property—the mysterious, forbidden woods where we were allowed to go only with a grownup because getting lost was so easy. From there came wood to fire Grandma's enormous cast-iron stove that took up a fourth of the kitchen, wood for the heating stove in the dining room, wood for the pot-bellied stove in the greenhouse and, once a central heating system was installed, wood for the furnace. Also in the woods were tree mushrooms which one of my uncles made into a delicious stew, butternuts by the bushelful, and an abundance of wild blackberries, red raspberries, gooseberries, boysenberries and thimbleberries. All that were not eaten out of the basket by children on the way home found their way to the table as pies, preserves, or ice cream toppings.

Particularly during the lean years of the Depression, these woods were often the only source of meat available to the family: rabbit, partridge, pheasant, quail, squirrel and an occasional porcupine (which, my father tells me, tastes like pork). A good muskrat pelt could bring $1.25, a large sum in those days and an important contribution to the family's always short supply of cash.

Meandering through the woods and crop land, eventually marking the boundary between our sweet corn and the neighboring dairyman's field corn, runs the little chortling stream that gives the road its name, Stony Brook.

The possibilities of this place, I'm sure, were not lost on my grandmother. She was accustomed to making do on a lot less than the farm promised. Surveying it with experienced eyes (40 years old, mother of seven with another on the way, forewoman of an agricultural crew in Italy before her marriage, and my grandfather's partner on the series of rented farms they'd been lucky enough to work in addition to their jobs in Utica's knitting mills), she recognized the business potential of the property. True, they were taking a gamble—borrowing money plus putting up all their savings of $500 to pay $4,500 for a rundown dairy farm at the beginning of the Depression. But to own productive land all around for as far as the eye could see was a dream come true—one they could never have attained back home. And, compared to the one-room, whitewashed stone dwelling where Grandma had grown up with her five sisters and one brother, the six-room house with barns and other outbuildings must have looked positively palatial.

So what if the blasts of winter rattled the small panes of

glass in the windows and whistled through the even then antique clapboards? There was plenty of wood and people to haul it. Who cared if the only running water gushed cold into a black cast-iron utility sink in the kitchen from the spout of a pump that needed to be worked by hand? There was plenty of water and no need to haul it. Couldn't afford to buy mattresses? Stuff your own with corn husks. Need pillows? Chickens were prized for their feathers almost as much as for their eggs. Nothing to wear? Grandma was a whiz with her 1914 treadle sewing machine and a few calico-printed flour sacks. Tired from picking strawberries all morning? Have a bowl of homemade macaroni, some lemonade, then take a little rest between the crisp, cool sheets of the bed in the back room before going out for the afternoon's work. Grandma always knew what to do to make things better.

My father calls it "Depression days resourcefulness," but I attribute my grandparents' optimistic spirit, their determination to live their lives well, to something deeper than the need to ride out a temporary slump in the world's economy. For even at its bleakest, the Depression here looked like up to them compared to the Italy they had left behind. On the farm, anyway, there was always the opportunity to obtain food, shelter, and a living, however modest, from the land. My grandparents were proud of their self-sufficiency and were willing to work day and night for it, having come from a long peasant tradition in which the worst shame of all is living off others.

Through my father and grandfather, I am an Italian citizen. By accident of birthplace, I am an American citizen. Until I was 10 years old, we lived almost always in neighborhoods that were pure Italy, just transported across the ocean, as Jerry Della Femina, the advertising executive, pointed out in his book, *An Italian Grows in Brooklyn*. Virtually everyone I knew was Italian, had grandmothers and grandfathers from Italy, and ate spaghetti on Thursdays and Sundays. Only when I began writing this book did it finally occur to me that my upbringing was really European, not American, in many ways. In a family where all the people who mattered (the old ones) constantly referred to the Old Country as though it were the "real" country, I suppose it was inevitable that I should feel, like them, as though this were a temporary stop—someplace to be taken advantage of and appreciated for what it was, but never to be confused with home.

Their way, our way, of making the best of it while we were here called for keeping alive a way of life that reaches back generations, the *civilità contadina* (Italian country life). Respect for the family is the foundation of that culture and thus the meaning of our family reunion. More than just a family party, more than just an excuse to overeat, it has become an annual confirmation, a renewal, of our identity.

None of this, by the way, was ever formally discussed or "taught" to us children. It was *assumed,* a given, as part of who you were that these were the attitudes and values you would adopt and live by. Had it not always been so? For me there were no feelings of being stifled by all this togetherness. On the contrary, it was a great comfort to be surrounded as a child by people who accepted you and cared for you just because you existed, not because you performed according to some external standard of excellence. We children were deeply cherished, every one, and if we got all A's, fine, very nice, but not necessary to win love or attention. Now that I have children of my own I, too, see the wisdom in this approach to child rearing. In many ways, I am becoming more like my mother and grandmother every day.

One thing is certain. After years of experimenting with other cuisines for other cookbooks and traveling the country lecturing about pregnancy nutrition, I keep coming back to our traditional home-made foods because they are among the world's best—the most appetizing, the most nutritious, the most economical. My older children, ages eight, seven and three, already knead the dough, stir the sauce and grate the cheese. The baby, age six months, yells to be held up high enough to watch what's going on! And around March every year they start to ask, "Mom, when will it be time to go to Grandma's to pick strawberries? When will we be going to the family reunion?"

This book is a treasury of the reunion recipes, many brought from the region around Bari and Alberobello, Italy by my grandmother and her friends, handed down to her daughters, daughters-in-law, nieces and cousins, and now entrusted to my generation. This is food in the classic Italian manner, from the country where the finest meals are to be had as a guest in someone's home. Everything is made by hand, fresh, from scratch. No corners are cut, because your family deserves the best and good food on the table comes first as a point of pride. In some cases this means taking time to prepare a complex dish, but not always. Cooking a bit of pasta and serving it with a ricotta sauce and a simple green salad takes but a few minutes, but what a delight!

Assembling and testing these recipes has not been accomplished without a lot of lively discussion in many people's kitchens. After a few years, cooks develop their own ways of doing certain things. An embellishment here, a seasoning there, a slightly different way with a crust: just enough of a change to make the dish their own. This is the reason cooking is such a personal art, such an evolutionary one. This book tries to put these later amendments aside in order to focus on the ingredients and methods my grandmother used in making the dishes that were standard fare for all of us. When controversy over garlic versus onions or yes, with anise, no, without erupted, the progress of the interview would be restored by asking (loudly), "But how did *Grandma* do it?" On that, there was always almost universal agreement.

Of all the people in our family who cook well, and there are many of them, probably my mother today cooks as close to

Grandma's way as anyone. Originally, to please my father; then, after Grandma died and my parents bought the farm from Grandpa, to satisfy him, a most exacting critic. His single criterion: Does it taste like Grandma's? Lately Mom has had to tolerate me sitting for months at the kitchen table, on and off, taking notes on everything she does, and asking why this, why that. She has been cooking this way for 37 years, time enough for it to have become second nature to her. Being asked to write down a recipe is a very difficult thing when it's really the process to which you're attuned: the way something looks, feels, smells, even *sounds* when it's right (this last sign is her way of telling when pasta is cooked just enough). She and my father have been drawn, willy-nilly, into this project as full collaborators. Without their unfailing patience and loving corrections at *every* turn, this book could never have been written. I would have been stuck more or less at the same place I was the first time I tried to make sauce on my own.

Standing in the center of my apartment kitchen, I tried to visualize what Mom did first, second, third—information gained during years of being around the kitchen, maybe making the salad or cleaning some vegetables while she made dinner. It was a pretty good technique. I remembered everything—except the part about browning the tomato paste in the meatball drippings and olive oil, the part that turns out to be *the key* to the special taste of our family sauce and something Mom learned, of course, from Grandma! Numerous incidents like this with other recipes as I was learning to cook for my own family soon made me realize that while I had assimilated *the ideas* about the importance of food preparation, I didn't know *the details* of how to make so many of the delicious foods I'd grown up on. Now I do, and the greatest satisfaction in presenting them in a book is the knowledge that they will be preserved, available for others to use long after those of us who took this food for granted have passed on.

A crucial element of these recipes is the ingredients

themselves. This, too, was a lesson learned only after some disappointing results in my first kitchen. By this time I was beginning a career as a college professor and not living in an Italian neighborhood. I cooked an Italian dish once or twice a week, using supermarket ingredients. Making the extra effort to travel half way across town to shop at an Italian specialty store seemed impossible to reconcile with the demands of my job. Still, when my parents were coming for a visit, I knew better than to put the shaker of already-grated Parmesan on the table! Then, I made the trip with pleasure, each time lingering long after I made my purchases just to take in the heady aromas of hanging sausages, whole forms of cheeses, tins of herbs and spices, strings of garlic bulbs and baskets of fresh-baked bread. It was like a trip home, back to the stores where Grandma had shopped for those few items she didn't make herself or for the imported Italian ingredients that gave certain dishes their unique flavor or texture.

Today, in larger supermarkets some of these ingredients are readily available in the deli department or in aisles given over to international foods. However, the best selection is still to be found at the neighborhood Italian specialty store where the proprietor is himself an importer or deals directly with one. Italian-grown semolina, Italian pasta, Italian plum tomatoes, Italian arborio rice are worth the difference in price for the distinction they bring to the dishes you prepare. Also, it's a place where homemade fresh sausage can be specially ordered if you don't feel like making your own and where you can obtain fine fresh ricotta without preservatives. Not many of us today view our kitchens as the total food processing centers Grandma did. We are much more likely to rely more on some ready-made components (cans of tomato paste, canned beans, cured sausage) which she simply could not afford to use. Since most of us are not in a position to grow our own food and put it up ourselves, making a friend of the Italian store proprietor is a step the entire family will appreciate. At the very least, the kids will enjoy the shopping trips.

If you live in an area where there are no Italian specialty stores, some stores in major cities offer mail order service. One such store, now being run by the third generation of the same family, is Manganaro's (488 Ninth Avenue—between 37th and 38th Streets—New York, New York 10018). In the imported Italian food business since 1893, Manganaro's prints an illustrated catalog, price list and order form. They also take orders by telephone: (212) LO 3-5331/2. Check the yellow pages of the telephone directories for large cities near you to find stores which advertise similar services, or contact the importers of Italian foods listed in the directory to find out which retail stores in your area carry Italian specialties.

Whether from supermarket deli or neighborhood Italian store, my basic shopping list includes:

• *Olive oil*—the real thing, not mixed with other oils. Try to find Sicilian oil whenever possible (it's a pale green and really tastes like olives). A more golden-colored variety comes from the area around Lucca (also good, but milder, tasting less distinctly of olives). Olive oil is also exported from Spain and Greece, so check the container to make sure it's Italian oil you're buying. A bit of this goes a long way in dressing a salad, and, since it's the primary cooking oil it adds a subtle richness to sauces, soups, roasts—even pizza dough. Invest in the gallon container to save money. Kept closed at room temperature, the oil won't become rancid even after months. If you become a more than 50 per cent Italian cook, you won't have to worry about this problem at all—a gallon will last only a couple of months, anyway.

• *Romano cheese*—again, the real thing, made from sheep's milk (the label should say "pecorino," sheep). Best to buy from a store that cuts your order from a wheel rather than

selling pre-wrapped pieces (you've no way of knowing
how long it's been cut). How to identify a superb piece?
It's been aged long enough to begin forming little beads of
oil within the body of the cheese and, while sharp and
assertive on the tongue, it leaves no harsh aftertaste (all
too common with domestic cow's milk "Romano," unfortunately). Buy in small quantities (what you will use in a
week or two) to insure the just barely crumbling texture
when you grate it. Refrigerators are notorious dehydrators,
so keep your cheese wrapped in a slightly damp cheesecloth inside a plastic bag. Grating the cheese just before
the spaghetti is served has always been my father's job.
Hearing my mother call him to do it is a sure sign that it's
time to come to the table!

• *Ricotta cheese*—traditionally, this very smooth, fine, even-
textured, moist cheese was derived from the whey left over
from the process of making other cheeses. Today it's much
more likely to be made of whole milk. Essential to recipes
for lasagne, manicotti, cannelloni and cheese ravioli, it also
stars as the main ingredient in white sauce for pasta and
the filling for cannolis. Sometimes called "Italian cottage
cheese," ricotta is *nothing whatever* like cottage cheese in
taste or performance in a recipe. Try to find a store that
sells fresh ricotta made on the premises and buy it the day
you plan to use it. Next best is to choose a packaged brand
that is made without preservatives. Anything that has a
shelf life of a week or more will stuff your pasta but not
add much to the flavor of your dish. Grandpa delivered
velvety fresh ricotta to the Italian stores in Utica once a
week when our family farm had a dairy operation, but his
specialty was *ricotta asciugante,* the Italian equivalent of
limburger. Fermented for months in large crocks, this hot,
sharp ricotta would be turned and turned until it reached a
dry, pasty consistency, then kneaded like bread dough

every two to three days. When appropriately concentrated (just spreadable) a dab of it would be enough to flavor an entire batch of pasta. Of course, as my father points out, it's one of those things you had to develop a taste for. A true peasant dish, *ricotta asciugante* sold for $1.50 a pound during the Depression when the price of fluid milk was bottoming out at 75 cents for a hundred-pound can!

• *Mozzarella cheese*—Everyone knows this cheese from its role as a pizza topping. In Southern Italy it's still made by hand from the milk of water buffalo (a common type of laboring animal there). Any domestic mozzarella will be made of cow's milk. Choose that made from whole milk as it melts more smoothly than the lowfat variety (a tendency toward rubbery strings). Mozzarella, mild and slightly springy to the bite, is an excellent teething cheese for babies.

• *Provolone cheese*—the mild variety (aged but a few months), sliced paper thin, clears the palate between bites of more forceful antipasti ingredients: hot peppers, spiced ham, pickled mushrooms, oil-cured olives, marinated artichokes. The aged variety (anywhere from a year to six or seven years) cut in thin slabs (not quite as mellow as in its younger days) is the perfect accompaniment to a hot, crusty Italian roll spread with butter. Some people also like to include it (cut in small pieces) in their homemade sausage. Provolone can be purchased in many amusing shapes, including piglets, melon balls and even certain popular saints. In blocks and balls, it can weight up to 200 pounds. This is the cheese you are most likely to see suspended from the rafters in an Italian market. On food shopping days the sliced provolone was the first white-wrapped package we'd open. The pound or so Mom bought would disappear by the next day—much eaten out of hand by us children—which was probably not a bad thing because once sliced, provolone dries out very rapidly, losing its creamy texture.

• *Olives*—black, oil-cured, and green with flakes of hot red pepper, usually put up in little white cardboard boxes with overlapping flaps for tops. Both used to accent the antipasti tray, by themselves as a snack, or (the black ones) cut up in slivers and scattered over the top of thick pizza. Kids tend to reject both of these kinds of olives, preferring the canned, pitted Californians they can slip over their fingertips to nibble off, one by one.

• *Meats*—fresh sausage (sweet and hot), cured sausage, pepperoni, salami, mortadella, capicolo, prosciutto, pancetta, pigs' feet: all are pork products processed and seasoned differently. Purchase *fresh sausage* when you haven't any homemade. Fresh means made that day to be used that day—without chemicals to "preserve" it, "enhance" flavor or "stabilize" color. If it's really fresh, these additives are completely unnecessary. If it's not fresh, buy elsewhere. Sweet means without red pepper; hot means with. In all cases, there should be *no* cereals in the sausage. *Cured sausage* (sweet or hot) is fresh sausage that has been dried under controlled conditions so that a certain percentage of its moisture is gone. Hot cured sausage, dried to the point of being very hard and stiff, is *pepperoni*. *Salami* differs from fresh sausage in that it contains more garlic and whole peppercorns, is ground much finer and is stuffed into a casing with almost double the diameter (about 4" across) of either coils or links of the fresh. Salami stands somewhere between fresh and pepperoni in moisture content and is usually served in thin slices on sandwiches or as part of an antipasti selection. The black peppercorns give it a characteristic bite that its smoked relative, *mortadella,* lacks. *Capicolo* is cooked ham with a coating of fiery red pepper and a thin casing which needs to be removed before the meat is eaten. The traditional shape is a cylinder about 10″ long with a diameter of 2½″. It is also served in thin slices cut across the diameter—one of my father's favorites for lunch. *Prosciutto,* an unsmoked, cured, heavily marbled ham with an almost crunchy crust of grated black pepper is the only one of these products that need not be refrigerated at the market. It frequently hangs from the ceiling of the market at room temperature. Prosciutto needs to be sliced down its longest side, so that it yields long, exquisitely thin strips for wrapping around melon slices, chunks of cheese, or fresh, sweet figs. It may also dress up an antipasto, flavor a dish of garden peas, wrap a bunch of asparagus, top a pizza or alternate with slices of veal in the classic saltimbocca. Very versatile, very expensive, very delicious. *Pancetta,* salt pork, is unsmoked, cured bacon used to flavor tomato and other pasta sauces and an occasional vegetable dish. If domestic, it may be too salty to use as is, so just blanch and proceed with your recipe. *Pigs' feet,* pickled in brine, were a favorite of my grandfather. Today they most commonly appear as a first course or as a dish to be served over the bar with beer. It seems there's always a glass jar of these tucked away in the back of my mother's refrigerator, but I must admit I've never summoned up enough courage to try one!

• *Semolina*—the golden, slightly grainy durum wheat flour with an exceptionally high proportion of gluten, the substance that makes it possible for pasta to hold its shape (and the reason so much domestic pasta turns to mush— see below). If you're going to make homemade pasta, use semolina rather than white flour to be really rewarded for your efforts. In a pinch, all-purpose unbleached flour also beats plain white flour. Never expect decent results with cake or pastry flour. Their soft, low-gluten characteristics make an unworkable dough that disintegrates in the cooking water. Semolina is the flour in all imported Italian pasta—the reason it maintains its character even when wed to the most high-spirited sauces.

• *Pasta*—from the basics (spaghetti, lasagne, ziti, shells, cannelloni, elbows) to the fantastic (fusilli, tortiglioni, bows, cappelletti, malfalde) and everything in between (acini di pepe, fettuccine, fettuccine verde, lumache, ravioli, tortellini). There are hundreds of variations of Italian-manufactured pasta, only a small number of which ever reach American shores. The closest domestic equivalents are the Buitoni high-protein line (semolina plus soy flour to complete the amino acid availability and boost the protein value to the point where it's an acceptable meat substitute on its own) and the Prince Superoni brand. There may be others made here from 100 percent durum wheat flour (it must say so on the package) available on a local or regional basis. Pasta made from hard wheat looks almost translucent before it's cooked, cooks through without turning to jelly on its surface, and adds flavor (not mere starchiness) to the dishes it appears in. *Egg noodles* are pasta with eggs in the dough. They are yellower and softer (and, therefore, quicker cooking) than plain pasta. Pasta may also include other ingredients, most often vegetables (spinach and artichokes are most common) that have been dried and ground or finely grated before being incorporated into the dough. Occasionally one finds some imported whole wheat pasta (brown because it contains the entire kernel of the wheat, germ and bran) which has a delightfully nutty taste—especially good as a side dish with game. Grandma used to buy her imported pasta in 20-pound boxes, a necessity in a house where pasta was served in some form or other every day.

• *Rice*—Italy has some of the best rice-growing land in the world, both in terms of the quality of the crop and the quantity produced. What I like best about buying Italian rice is the off-white linen-like bag it comes in, complete with a red drawstring and metal tag. The kids like to make these into little hand puppets. Inside the bag, the grains of rice shine like tiny pearls. As they cook, they plump up but don't stick together, much the way domestic brown rice behaves. Grandma always used this rice in her chicken soup and I also enjoy it in chicken stuffing, rice pudding, and as a baby food (cooked in broth with a sprinkle of grated Romano). Your risotto alla Milanese will be a standout when you use Italian rice.

• *Anchovies*—to flavor certain sauces, to run in strips across a pizza, to accent an antipasti tray, nothing beats a few of these. As children we would resist these on pizza (a touch my father insisted upon). The compromise: Mom would make one plain, one with anchovies, and since the plain one would disappear in a few minutes and there would always be some of the anchovy left, anybody who wanted some re-heated the next day had to endure the anchovies. In my case, love of pizza overcame my dislike of anchovies and I wound up learning to appreciate them almost as much as my father does.

• *Tomatoes*—canned, plum tomatoes for sauce (most marked "San Marzano" variety) packed in crushed tomatoes, tomato juice or water. Peeled or not, as you prefer (in tomatoes picked at the peak of ripeness, the skins are so thin and soft they dissolve in sauce, anyway). At the Italian store you may be able to buy by the case and save 15-20 percent over supermarket single can prices. This brings the cost per can right into line with what's charged for domestic, non-plum tomatoes and puree. Do Italian plum tomatoes really taste that much different? I think so. Even the canned ones have an air of garden freshness about them. If your market doesn't carry the kind imported from Italy, the California-grown "tipo Italiano" that show the plum tomatoes on the label illustration are your best bet. *Tomato paste,* also made from plum tomatoes, is usually stocked at the Italian store. An intensifier of the color and taste of your sauce, tomato paste must be diluted with water as it's added to the sauce, then simmered along with the other ingredients until all is in harmony. Paste alone does not a sauce make. Tomatoes, several different varieties, were a major part of life on Grandma's farm. Grandpa sowed the seed from last year's plants in his greenhouse every year on St. Joseph's Day (March 19), thus starting a new crop cycle. Grandma put up literally hundreds of quarts of tomatoes every summer to be used throughout the year in sauce. She also made her own paste (*conserva*), boiling tomatoes down over a wood fire in the side yard fireplace on hot summer days. My mother continues to can her own tomatoes, but buys paste. I, living with just a summer salad garden, buy both.

There are many, many other items for sale in Italian stores: specialty items, coffees, candies, pastry shells, ready-to-use antipasti and side dishes, kitchen equipment, nuts, seasonings, flavorings, cookies, brandied fruits, ice cream desserts, wines, herb teas, and breads. Many of these items you'll be able to make yourself with the recipes in this book. Others you'll want to sample as supplements to your basic menu plans. Either way, shopping the Italian neighborhood store is a small way of keeping in touch with one's culinary roots or exploring the diversity of another cuisine. Even for those members of our family who get along with what's available in the supermarket for most of the year, a trip to the Italian store is the first step in preparing for the annual reunion.

Early on the morning of the reunion members of the committee arrive to dig the roasting pit and get the wood fire or charcoal going so that my Uncle Fred's steamer can be started, begin preparing the clams, put up the tent in case of rain, set up the picnic tables, arrange the beer, soda and milk in tubs of cracked ice, take charge of the growing band of children—all in a state of high excitement—and help put the finishing touches on the foods before arranging them on the serving table. Around noon, the rest of the family starts to drive up, each group toting its own dish to share, the cars ultimately lining the road all the way to Uncle Fred's. Somebody turns on the record player, and, to the strains of "Oh, Marie!" we're off on a wonderful day of talking, eating, arguing, eating, singing, eating, telling all the old family stories, then eating again. Without a doubt, the best day of the year!

My father's cousin, Lena Virgilio Tomaino, sparked my interest in writing this book with a chance remark at a reunion about 10 years ago. Coming around the corner of the house and seeing the reunion table fully set with the array of marvelous dishes everyone had brought, she said, "It's a shame we're all watching our figures so these days. Everything looks so beautiful. Nobody cooks like this anymore. *This is the way we used to eat!*"

And, I think it's fair to say, the way we used to be.

Doing the meat
to a turn over the roasting pit

2

Antipasti

TECHNICALLY SPEAKING, "antipasto" means before the pasta. Here, though, I've included all the dishes we nibble on in the morning before the main meal is served on reunion day. Most of these help to fortify the men working around the roasting pit, laying the fire and loading the steamer with clams, just-picked sweet corn and chickens. For many, the clams are the high point of the day. One dozen usually makes a serving, but I've seen true clam lovers pack away eight or ten dozen without even trying!

A few years ago, Uncle Fred solved a big reunion problem: how to do clams for over a hundred people. He designed and made a 30-gauge sheet steel steamer. Its bottom rests on the grill, close to the red-hot coals of the wood fire. Inside are racks adjustable to several levels. Clams go on the bottom rungs, corn and chicken on the upper two. In the very bottom, enough water to send up a continuous cloud of steam. As one batch is done, another is put in: plain steamed clams, clams on the grill—whatever suits your pleasure. All the men stand around, offering opinions about how to do each step, but the real expert is Uncle Fred. He relishes his work. Yelling out orders, making loud jokes, always in a gleeful mood, he sets the tone for the whole day. His sense of humor is infectious. As a child, I was scared to death of him—afraid of his loud voice, afraid he'd single me out of the gang of kids for some special joking attention. Later, I began to appreciate his upbeat approach to life. He's able to take pleasure in the day-to-day events so many of us overlook. Freddy, everybody says, is the life of the party. That's true, but he also takes some of the party back into life, spreading good will and raising people's spirits wherever he goes. Today, I know his is a rare spirit in a hard, unfeeling world. With Uncle Fred presiding, it's no wonder the roasting pit is a lively spot people gravitate to all day long!

Our clam recipes follow, and since you probably won't be doing them for more than a hundred people, I've listed ingredients to serve four. Any of these can also be used for oysters, which we also love (Grandpa grew up near Taranto, site of some of the world's most legendary oyster beds).

Clam Preparation

Preparing clams to be eaten raw or cooked begins the day before the celebration. To get rid of the sand that clings to the shell, scrub the exterior (this also gives you a chance to make sure that every clam is closed tight—discard any that are not). Place scrubbed clams in a large tub and sprinkle liberally with a layer of cornmeal. Repeat, layering in cornmeal, until all clams are covered. Add ice to fill tub and let sit overnight. This corn meal bath allows the whole clam to be eaten without having to clean the stomachs. In all cases, the clams we're talking about are cherrystones.

Clams on the Half Shell

Remove clams from ice and corn meal bath. Rinse under cold water. Insert sharp knife through muscle and remove top half of shell. Eat out of hand after sprinkling with a bit of vinegar, or arrange on a tray of ice with seafood sauce nearby for people to serve themselves.

Our standard sauce for raw clams, oysters, or shrimp cocktail:

Seafood Sauce

⅔ cup ketchup
⅓ cup grated horseradish
⅛ teaspoon black pepper

Combine all ingredients in a small mixing bowl. Makes one cup, enough to season about four dozen clams.

Clams on the half shell keep us going while we're waiting for the other clams to get finished!

Steamed Clams

My favorites, though I didn't discover that I liked them until I was 20 years old!

4 dozen clams, ready to cook (see p. 24)
2 cups water
melted salted butter

In a large kettle (eight-quart, if you have it), place water and unopened clams. Put kettle over high heat until water boils and steam forms. Cover, turning heat down until vapor just continues to escape. When clams open, remove with tongs or a gloved hand (you'll be able to grip the shell, but they are extremely hot). Serve at once on a platter. At each place, put a small bowl or cup of melted butter to dip the clams in—the only sauce these need!

Joe's Clams Casino

My father is very fussy about doing these right, so, naturally, people keep asking for more. Too much breading kills the flavor of the clams or oysters. Too little, and the crumbs turn gritty.

3 dozen clams, ready to cook (see p. 24)
6 thin slices Italian Bread, preferably homemade (see
    p. 65)
2 teaspons parsley flakes *or* 1 teaspoon chopped
    fresh parsley
⅓ cup grated Romano cheese
½ teaspoon oregano
½ teaspoon garlic salt
¼ teaspoon black pepper
Olive oil

Open clams, draining off most of the juice and discarding the top shell. Arrange on large baking sheet so edges just touch.

In a large mixing bowl, crumble the bread very fine. Add seasonings and enough oil to bind the mixture. Stir thoroughly. Spread a thin layer of breading on top of each clam.

Bake in the middle of the oven at 350° until the breading is lightly browned, approximately 20 minutes. Watch these carefully so as not to overbake, otherwise the crust will be hard and the clams tough.

Clams on the Grill

These can be done almost anywhere with a minimum of fuss.

4 dozen clams, ready to cook (see p. 24)
⅛ pound salted butter

Arrange clams or oysters, unopened, on grill placed low over live coals. As the shells open, the clam will adhere to the cooler (upper) surface. Turn them over, slipping ¼ teaspoon of butter into each one. When the butter begins to sizzle (after a minute or two at the most), remove from the grill. Handle with tongs or a gloved hand as shells are intensely hot and cool very slowly! Serve hot in the shells.

Fried Peppers and Onions

Cooking this brings back memories of midday meals at Grandma's when I visited over my summer vacation. Peppers and onions, pulled fresh from the garden, served as a side dish or sandwich filling (see next recipe) were staples in that household. When cooked slowly, the onions do not brown and the oil does not smoke, so serve with the oil as a dressing—so good to eat, even after the vegetables are gone, by dipping in a chunk of homemade bread.

> ⅓ cup olive oil
> 1 clove garlic, peeled
> 4 cups sweet green peppers (Italian variety, if
>   possible), in strips
> 1½ cups thinly sliced onions
> Salt and pepper

In a large frying pan, sauté the garlic in oil over medium heat until golden brown. Discard garlic. Add peppers and onions and cook, covered, until peppers are soft. Cool to room temperature. Serve with cooking oil drizzled over the vegetables. Add salt and pepper to taste. Serves 4.

Pepper and Egg Sandwich

A way to have Fried Peppers and Onions for lunch, even if you're not going to be home for the meal!

1 small loaf Italian Bread (see p. 65) *or* 4 Italian rolls
4 tablespoons butter
4 eggs, beaten
1 recipe Fried Peppers and Onions (above)
Salt and pepper

Slice bread or rolls lengthwise. If sandwich is to be eaten right away, warm bread, opened, in 250° oven until you're ready to fill it.

In a large frying pan, melt butter over low heat. Add eggs and let cook until they begin to thicken. Stir in fried peppers and onions, drained of most of their cooking oil. Continue to stir until ingredients are well combined and the eggs are firm, but not dry. Lift out with spatula and arrange on one half of bread or rolls. Salt and pepper to taste. Wrap in foil for a hearty workingman's lunch, a tasty alternative to cold cuts. Serves 4.

Another way to slice the bread to serve four: cut into eight slices and fill each sandwich with some of the filling. Save the heels of the bread to use for bread crumbs.

These sandwiches, along with some cold beers, keep the crowd around the roasting pit satisfied until the main meal is served at two o'clock.

Frittata with Greens

A country omelet that can't be beat when the eggs are fresh from the hen and the greens just dug from the lawn! Grandma kept chickens in order to sell eggs as well as for the meat they provided. No antibiotics, hormones, or 24-hour laying schedules for those birds. And were those eggs delicious! Grandma also never could understand products like "weed 'n' feed" for the yard. Dandelion greens were a welcome addition to the diet—one of the first fresh salad possibilities of spring after a long winter of canned vegetables. Though we children didn't understand the finer points of nutrition in those days, we liked dandelions because they were pretty. Even when they were presented in a wilted condition after being stuck in a dress pocket for a few hours, our mothers thought so, too.

> 2 pounds dandelion or similar greens (spinach, Swiss chard, etc.)
> ½ cup olive oil
> 1 clove garlic, peeled
> 3 eggs, beaten
> ¼ cup grated Romano cheese
> Salt and pepper

In a large saucepan, boil greens until they are tender and all bitterness is gone. Drain. Transfer to a frying pan and sauté over low heat with oil and garlic for 30 minutes. Discard garlic.

In a small mixing bowl, combine eggs and cheese. Add egg mixture to greens in frying pan. Stir over moderate heat until eggs are firm, but not dry. Salt and pepper to taste. Serve hot. Serves 4.

Grandma's Dill Pickles

To accompany the sandwiches and clams, little dishes of marinated and pickled vegetables are set out around noon. It's possible to buy many of these things ready-made in the Italian specialty store today, but the ones we make ourselves really do have a superior flavor. It's possible to do these even if you have only a small amount of food storage space: just do two jars at a time, instead of 20!

Grandma's dill pickles were famous. Was it the well water she used to pack them in? Maybe. Now that my parents own the farm, Mom's pickles taste exactly like Grandma's, though Grandma kept hers in the cellar in a huge earthenware crock with a wooden lid.

> 8-10 fresh-picked, young cucumbers (3 to 5 inches
>   long)
> 3 cloves garlic, peeled
> 3 sprigs fresh dill
> 1 cup water
> ½ cup white vinegar
> 1 tablespoon salt

Scrub cucumbers thoroughly under cold running water. Pack closely, but do not squeeze, into a quart glass jar containing the garlic and dill.

In a saucepan, bring water, vinegar and salt to boil. Pour into jar, making sure to cover the ends of the cucumbers and stopping ½ inch from the top of the jar. Cool to room temperature. Store for 6 weeks before using. Makes one quart jar.

Roasted Peppers

12 large sweet peppers (red or green), washed
1½ cups olive oil (approximately)
Salt

Place peppers on rack of grill, under broiler, or spear each in turn with a fondue or other long-handled fork and hold over stovetop burner. Turn peppers gradually, moving them when the surface begins to blister and blacken, but not the flesh beneath. When an entire pepper is done, set it aside, on its top, to cool.

When cool enough to handle, remove and discard top, inner membranes, seeds, and charred skin. Cut pepper in half. Lightly salt each half, then lay flat in a pint glass canning jar. Drizzle enough oil over each half to cover it before you add the next. Fill jar to within an inch of the top, then add additional oil to insure that peppers are completely covered. Seal and store at room temperature. Makes two pint jars. Serve as part of an antipasti tray, in a tossed salad, or as a side dish with meats.

Frank Argento's Pickled Eggplant

The Argentos are our cousins by marriage. Frank's father married my grandfather's cousin, Antonia. My father is the godfather for Frank and Carmella's son, Nicky, now a man my age with children of his own. When we lived in Utica, we saw them often. In fact, I have a scar on my forehead from the time I fell in their kitchen, grazing my head on a sharp, square table leg. We kids had been getting wilder and wilder the longer the grownups talked, and my mother's repeated warnings to stop running around and around the table had fallen on deaf ears (isn't it always this way?). So, I was curious to return to the scene of the accident 30 years after it happened to see how things had changed. Remarkably, hardly at all—the well, the spot where the tall windmill stood, the second kitchen for canning—the table still located right in the middle of the kitchen! This time, it was my turn to do some of the talking, and when we got around to food, Frank insisted on feeding me supper. (I was seven months pregnant at the time, and I think he had an idea that I might not get a meal on the plane I was taking back to New York that night—he was right.) I never even knew he cooked.

Out came the homemade sausage patties, an offer of wine, some salad—and these excellent pickled antipasti. A warm and friendly meal, so much nicer than one could ever find in a restaurant at any price. And all on the spur of the moment. Thanks, Frank. Thanks, Carmella. It was great!

> 2 small eggplants, washed but not peeled
> 2 cups water
> 1 cup white wine vinegar
> ½ teaspoon salt
> ¼ teaspoon oregano
> ¼ teaspoon garlic powder
> ⅛ teaspoon red pepper flakes
> 1 cup olive oil (approximately)

Cut eggplant into slices about ¼ inch thick, then cut each slice into ½-inch-wide strips.

In large saucepan, combine water and vinegar and bring to full boil. Drop in eggplant strips, bring to boil and simmer for two minutes. Drain and cool to the point where the eggplant is slightly warm to the touch. Squeeze out excess vinegar/water by pressing down on the eggplant with your hands or the back of a large spoon. Discard liquid.

In medium mixing bowl combine eggplant and seasonings. Add olive oil, making sure the eggplant is covered. Let stand until eggplant is saturated with oil. Lift out strips and pack in pint glass canning jars. Add oil needed to cover eggplant, stopping about ½ inch from the top of the jar. Seal and store at room temperature. Serve as an antipasto or as a side dish with sausage. Makes two pint jars.

Carmella Argento's Pickled Peppers

These complement Frank's eggplant beautifully.

3 cups peppers (sweet or hot), cut in strips
1 clove garlic, peeled
1 tablespoon salt
1 teaspoon sugar
¼ teaspoon alum
½ cup water
½ cup vinegar

Place peppers, garlic, salt, sugar and alum in a quart glass canning jar.

In a saucepan, combine water and vinegar and bring to full boil. Pour vinegar water over contents of jar, stopping ½ inch from top. Seal. Cool. to room temperature. Store six weeks before serving. Makes one quart.

Lampasciuni alla Barese (Marinated Shallots)

3 cups shallots
Water
2 tablespoons salt
¾ cup olive oil
¼ cup vinegar
1 clove garlic, peeled
1 teaspoon oregano

Remove and discard the outer membrane of the shallots. In a large saucepan, cover the shallots with water. Bring to a boil, then add salt. Simmer over moderate heat until tender. Drain and rinse several times with cold water. Pack loosely in a quart glass canning jar.

In a small mixing bowl, combine oil, vinegar, garlic and oregano to make a marinade. Pour into the jar, covering the shallots completely. Seal and let stand at room temperature overnight. Store in refrigerator. When served, shallots should taste sweet. Makes one quart jar.

Stuffed Hot Cherry Peppers

The hotter, the better is the rule in picking peppers for this dish. I remember watching in horrified amazement as grownups took bites, sucked in air through clenched teeth, let out a groan as though punched in the stomach, then grabbed frantically for glasses of cold ice water or beer to cut the sting. This meant the peppers were perfect! Repeat performances were standard for all that because, as my mother explains, these taste *so good*. Witnessing these scenes as a child prepared my mind for an understanding of masochism later in life.

The setting for many of these hot pepper binges was the kitchen of Phil and Mary Rosello, friends so close they seemed like family to me. On Friday nights my parents, the Rosellos, the Taverneses, and the Sansones would get together for cards. The children were brought along as a matter of course (I can count on my fingers the number of times a babysitter was ever employed by our family). When we got tired, we'd just throw ourselves on top of the mountain of coats on Phil and Mary's bed and go to sleep, rousing for a moment only when the excitement over a particular game crescendoed to an ear-splitting level. Or when the peppers were brought out around midnight (as a pick-me-up to keep everyone playing until three or four in the morning), and the oooh-ing and ahh-ing and gasping for water began.

The Friday night card parties ceased during my high school years, replaced for a time by early Sunday morning golf matches (men only), then by seeing each other at the round of weddings for all the girls (10 in all). Phil is gone now after a long battle with cancer, but whenever we have these peppers we recall his standard line, "I know I'm gonna regret this tomorrow, but I gotta have *just one more!*"

> 16 hot cherry peppers
> 6 slices Italian bread, including crust
> 2 ounces anchovies, diced (salt packed or oil packed)
> 2 tablespoons grated Romano cheese
> ½ teaspoon parsley flakes *or* 1 teaspoon chopped
>   fresh parsley
> ¼ teaspoon oregano
> Salt and pepper to taste
> Olive oil
> Water

Cut off stem ends of peppers and remove inner membranes and seeds. Wash and dry inside and out. Cut bread into small cubes and combine with anchovies, cheese, parsley, oregano, salt and pepper in a large mixing bowl. If the anchovies are oil-packed, add the packing oil, then as much olive oil as needed to bind the mixture together.

Spoon the mixture into the peppers, then arrange on a shallow baking dish or pie plate so their sides just touch. Add water to a depth of ¼ inch in the bottom of the pan. Bake in the middle of the oven at 375° for 20 minutes or until tops are browned. Cool to slightly warmer than room temperature before serving.

Lupini Beans

Kids enjoy splitting these open with their teeth (the skins become softened by the salt processing) and squirting the bean into their mouths by pressing on it with the thumb and forefinger. About the only sign left at our house that there have been lupini beans around is the pile of discarded, creamy skins in the center of the kitchen table. And the stream of requests for drinks of water for several hours after the feed!

    5 pounds lupini beans, dry
    5 cups salt
    Water

In a large kettle, place beans and ½ cup salt. Cover with water, refrigerate, and let soak two days. Drain beans and remove any broken or discolored ones. Rinse and drain again.

Add ½ cup more salt to beans. Cover with fresh cold water and bring to boil. Simmer until tender. Let stand until cooled to room temperature. Drain. Add ½ cup more salt and cover with fresh cold water. Drain and rinse each day for the next seven days, covering each time with fresh water and another ½ cup salt. The beans are done when they are no longer bitter. To store, fill a glass quart canning jar ¾ full of beans and cover with salt water (ratio: ⅓ cup salt to one gallon water). Makes 3 quarts. Seal lids and store in refrigerator.

Antipasto, Linda's Way

My sister, Linda, makes the antipasto everyone wants at all family parties. It's what people have in mind when they think of the word antipasto—an artfully arranged tray of raw vegetables and a selection of Italian meats and cheeses, lightly dressed with olive oil, wine vinegar and seasonings. Linda thinks you shouldn't try to put everything on an antipasto tray. She prefers a few ingredients so each can be especially savored. Of course, the range of possible combinations is limited only by one's imagination and personal preference. Her favorite comes to the reunion table, heralding the beginning of the main meal.

1 head lettuce
2 tomatoes, cut in wedges, *or* 1 cup cherry tomatoes
1 cucumber, peeled and sliced in rounds
2 celery stalks, cut in quarters
¼ pound hard salami, sliced thin
¼ pound capicolo, sliced thin
¼ pound provolone, sliced thin
1 cup oil-cured black olives (imported)
8 marinated artichoke hearts
8 scallions

OPTIONAL:

2 hard-boiled eggs, sliced
8 hot cherry peppers
8 anchovy fillets
½ cup pimento, sliced in strips
1 large green pepper, sliced in thin rounds

Dressing:

6 tablespoons olive oil
2 tablespoons red wine vinegar
1 teaspoon garlic salt
¼ teaspoon oregano, dried
Salt and pepper to taste

Arrange lettuce leaves on large platter, then place other ingredients in an attractive pattern on top of the lettuce. Sprinkle with a bit of cold water and cover to refrigerate if antipasto is not to be served right away.

Combine all ingredients for dressing in a bowl or shaker. Mix thoroughly and spoon over antipasto. Serve at once. Serves 8.

Making maccheroni
in Grandma's Kitchen

3

Pasta, Pizza & Bread

*N*O MATTER whether the dough was for pasta, pizza, bread, pie or pastry, it shared a common destiny: to be kneaded, rolled, patted and shaped on Grandma's bread board. Designed to fit exactly over the white enameled top of the old kitchen table, Grandpa nailed it together in 1930 out of two inch-thick, one foot by three feet pine boards and it saw almost daily use for the next 35 years. Not much to look at, perhaps, by today's hard-rock-maple-butcher-block-laminate standards, its worn surface bears testimony to the hours and hours Grandma spent working on it. In each corner, deep scoring from the passes of knives through rolls of dough for fettucine, tagliatelle or lasagne. Across the bottom edge, a virtual feathering from cutting strips of pasta into the tiny bits that Grandma would roll over her thumbtip to form *orecchiette* (little ears). At the center, a spot so smooth from constant friction that even the grain of the wood has been erased.

Grandma was not a tall person. Grandpa's U.S. naturalization papers give his height as 5′4″; Grandma came up to his shoulder, if that (all the semi-ceremonial photographs of them taken on various holidays, standing side by side, show Grandma with her black two-inch heels on, making it hard to tell for sure). For all she would have admired their looks, Grandma would have been out of place standing next to today's Formica counters and islands. The bread board turned sideways to straddle the end of the kitchen table was just the right height for her. And it's in this position, bent just slightly at the waist, her hands flying, rolling out the pasta to such a thinness that she could have had a career as a professional *sfoglina* in a restaurant somewhere, that she comes most clearly into my memory. I loved watching her do this, sitting around the table in the coolness of an early summer morning before the heat of the day made it around to the north side of the house, sometimes in the company of my cousins, sometimes just Grandma and me. I love doing it today, my own children grouped around the table clamoring for bits of dough to roll out for their own little pizzas. Relegated for 15 years to the ignominy of the corn crib after Mom and Dad renovated the house, Grandma's bread board is now back in service in my kitchen. Every time I use it, I remember Grandma and wonder what thoughts crossed her mind as she stood, day after day, pushing and pulling, turning and squeezing, flouring and shaking, turning out that magnificent dough.

PASTA

Handmade Pasta

This is termed handmade, rather than homemade, because you can put dough through a pasta machine at home and have homemade pasta, but you won't have this! You also won't have the sensual delight of working the dough with your hands, feeling it achieve elasticity and seeing its texture turn from crumbly to glossy due solely to your efforts. Try to make pasta on days with low humidity so you'll encounter fewer problems with dough sticking to the work surface and to itself when you cut it into strips. Also, low humidity is a help in drying the pasta thoroughly if you plan to store part of your batch. Grandma's method: Spread a freshly laundered sheet over a bed and lay out your finished pasta there to dry overnight.

Aunt Esther is our biggest pasta maker these days, and it wouldn't be a reunion without some of her terrific noodles.

3½ to 4 cups semolina or unbleached flour
    (approximately)
4 eggs
1 tablespoon salt
¼ cup cold water (approximately)
Olive oil (just enough to coat your hands)
8 quarts water, at full rolling boil

On a large pastry board, smooth countertop or in a very large mixing bowl, make a mound with 3 cups of the semolina or unbleached flour. Hollow out the center of the mound and put the eggs and salt into it. Beat the eggs and salt together a bit with a fork; then, using your hands, move flour from the outside edges of the mound into the middle, filling the well and beginning to combine flour, eggs and salt. Continue working the ingredients together until all the flour is absorbed by the eggs and the dough forms a somewhat soft, almost crumbly ball. Depending on how much moisture is in the semolina or flour you are using, how big your eggs are, and how humid a day it is, you may need to add a few teaspoonsful of water to the dough to bring it to the soft ball stage. However, the dough should remain on the dry side, not sticky.

Scatter some of the remaining semolina or flour on the work surface and knead dough 10 to 15 minutes until it becomes very soft, smooth, glossy and elastic. How elastic? Enough so that when you take a piece of dough, roll it into a pencil shape and pull on both ends, then let go, it pulls back to its original size in slow motion as though it has a life of its own. Oil your hands very lightly and pat surface of dough ball, then transfer to large bowl and cover with damp towel. Let rest one hour at room temperature.

To roll out, lightly dust work surface with semolina or flour again. Divide dough ball into at least two pieces as the mass spreads far and wide when it's rolled as thin as it should be. Place one dough ball on floured surface and cover others with dampened cloth. Flatten the first piece into an oblong shape by tamping it down with the heel of your hand. Try to keep the oblong shape as you work, extending it lengthwise, then crosswise, with strokes of the rolling pin (Grandma used the standard Italian straight one that resembles a fat broomhandle, but any rolling pin will do). The goal is to insure an even thickness throughout without pressing down so hard with the rolling pin that the dough gets stuck or starts to tear. If the sheet should start to stick, lift it gently with a spatula and dust underneath with a bit more flour. When your oblong of dough is paper-thin, dust it sparingly with flour and let rest 10 to 15 minutes, or until it feels slightly dry to the touch. This step is important because if the dough is too sticky, the next step will be impossible.

Roll the oblong as you would a jellyroll, and quickly cut

crosswise into strips with a very sharp, *non-serrated edge* knife. Unroll strips at once and set them aside on waxed paper or muslin to dry for at least an hour. Move noodles about so both sides dry. Repeat all procedures with remaining pieces of the original dough ball. Depending on how wide you cut the strips, you will have:

>FETTUCCINE (¼ inch wide)
>TAGLIATELLE (⅜ inch wide)
>LASAGNE (1½ to 2 inches wide)

If you buy special cutting devices, you can also make:

>RAVIOLI—to stuff with cheese or meat
>PAPPARDELLE—curly edges

and other flat pastas. This recipe makes a pound of pasta, enough to serve four hungry people as a main course, or eight people as a side dish.

To cook handmade pasta, remember that the softer the dough and the thinner the noodle, the less cooking time is required. This pasta swells up also, making it even more important to roll it out extremely thin. Otherwise, you can wind up with a bowl of thick, half-cooked noodles after all your hard work! To cook one pound, bring 4 quarts of water to a full, rolling boil. Salt to taste. Add pasta and cook 2 to 4 minutes, depending on thickness. To check doneness, lift out a strand or two and taste it. It should be cooked through, but not mushy, termed *al dente*. Serve on heated plates after draining in colander or lifting out, bit by bit, with two forks. Whatever sauce you choose should be thoroughly incorporated into the pasta while it's still in the serving dish, not just plopped on top. The same goes for any added ingredients (vegetables, bits of meat or seafood) you use to vary your pasta dishes. Grated Romano cheese is the classic garnish. For some sparkling ideas about pasta combinations, consult: *Pasta and Pizza* (New York: St. Martin's Press, 1979).

Orecchiette

These traditional Apulian macaroni shells were Grandma's specialty. Each one forms a little pocket to hold the sauce so each bite is a juicy delight. To shape these, follow the recipe above for Handmade Pasta. After cutting dough into ½-inch-wide strips, cut off ½-inch-long bits and stretch each over your thumb while rolling your thumb on the work surface. The movement looks as though you're leaving your thumbprint, but it actually curls the dough ever so slightly. Set aside on waxed paper or muslin and dry overnight. Follow the cooking directions above for Handmade Pasta. We children loved these with plain butter and grated cheese (kids seem to go through a phase where tomato sauce is absolutely out!). Grownups like them with a simple ricotta sauce. A hearty meat sauce is also a fitting accompaniment, especially on freezing winter days. When Grandma asked, "Do you want a bowl of macaroni?," this is what she meant. Invariably it was served with Grandpa's wine.

One measure of a man of my grandfather's generation was the wine he made for his family. Grandpa set great store by his. With the sparkle and color of rubies, full-bodied, yet mellow—a close relative of the Primitivo produced in his native region of Apulia—it proclaimed him a prince. Though we were not a hard-drinking lot (three to four hundred gallons a year were nothing to some Italian families of our acquaintance), we drank at least a hundred gallons of Grandpa's finest from December to December, most of it as the perfect complement to Grandma's midday pasta.

At the table, the bottle of wine was always placed directly in front of Grandpa's plate. He poured for everyone in their turn. We children were offered a little bit diluted about half and half with water, a mixture that rarely provoked requests for seconds. It wasn't until I was in my twenties that I began to cultivate a taste for wine and, long after he stopped making it, started to respect Grandpa's virtuosity as a vintner.

The year of Grandma and Grandpa's fiftieth wedding anniversary was the last that Grandpa made wine. At every reunion since, we've sampled other wines, but the verdict is always the same: pleasant enough, but nowhere near Grandpa's. It added warmth, beauty, and (the *paesani* maintained) good digestion to family meals. I look forward to the day when I'll have Grandpa's old press refitted, order some grapes, and, using his traditional methods, fill the family wine cellar once again.

Pasta Verde
Pasta Bruni

For a change from yellow pasta, spinach or whole wheat flour can be substituted for some of the semolina or unbleached flour used in the recipe for handmade pasta. The resulting dough is either green or brown.

For Pasta Verde, add ¾ pound spinach, cooked, thoroughly drained and chopped *very fine,* to the eggs and salt in the well before you start combining the flour.

For Pasta Bruni, substitute half whole wheat flour for half the semolina or unbleached flour. This dough will be considerably softer than standard pasta, takes a while longer to dry, and a shorter time to cook (stay right there while it's cooking because it will be done in a flash). Pasta bruni is exceptional as a side dish with game.

Spaghetti

Spaghetti and all other macaroni with a round shape or holes are manufactured commercially by means of an extruding machine. The dough is fed into a large container, then forced under pressure through the attachments that form certain shapes. In action, the effect is like hair growing very fast out of someone's scalp. As the spaghetti (or: elbows, penne, mostaciolli, cannelloni, rigatoni, manicotti, perciatelli, capellini, ziti, fusilli, etc.) reaches the desired length, it's cut, transferred to a drying area, then packaged. These shapes can also be accomplished with a home pasta machine by outfitting it with the attachments you require. When using these machines, it is best to follow the manufacturer's recipes as each machine has slightly different ways of working the dough through the feeder mechanism—and cleaning the extruding attachment is hard enough without trying to contend with a mass of hopelessly clogged dough.

Grandma purchased Italian imported pasta as an alternative to the egg pasta she made herself. She stored the 20-pound boxes in the back bedroom—always keeping several varieties on hand. I suppose most people recognize pasta as the Italian answer to the potato as a starchy staple in the diet, but few are aware of the literally thousands of variations possible in serving it. Depending on the type of noodle selected, the sauce, and the vegetables, meat or seafood added to the dish, it can be as simple as a plate of spaghetti dressed with oil and garlic or as elaborate as baked lasagne, a multi-layered creation with meat and cheeses. In Grandma's household, a day without pasta at least once would have been unthinkable. And, for all that it's become a cliché, an enormous platter of spaghetti and meatballs is still the centerpiece of our family's reunion table.

An enormous literature has developed about the correct

way to cook spaghetti and other non-egg pastas. These noodles are harder than egg pasta and so require more cooking time. However, they are still tested for doneness the same way: firm to the bite *(al dente),* but cooked through. It's impossible to give a time for each shape (much depends on how much water you're cooking in—allow four quarts to each pound of pasta, when you add the salt, whether you add all the pasta at once, the type of heat you use—gas or electric, and the kettle you're using—aluminum, stainless steel, enamel). The thinner the body of the noodle, the shorter time needed. In general, the finest strands (capelli, spaghettini) should be checked at least three minutes after the water returns to a boil, spaghetti at seven minutes, and thick noodles like malfalde and lasagne after 10 minutes. Test every minute or so thereafter to prevent overcooking.

Our way with spaghetti goes like this:

> 1 pound spaghetti
> 4 quarts water
> 2 tablespoons salt
> 2 tablespoons oil (optional)

In a very large kettle, bring water to full, rolling boil. Add salt and all of spaghetti at one time. Oil added now will prevent strands from sticking and clumping together. Stirring spaghetti often also helps.

When spaghetti is done, turn out all at once into a large colander. Most of the water rushes out immediately. To get rid of the rest (it will dilute your sauce if you don't), grasp the handles of the colander and flip the spaghetti upward and over on itself repeatedly until all water droplets cease.

Turn out onto a large platter or into a large serving bowl. Toss with the sauce of your choice and add grated Romano cheese over the top. Pass extra grated cheese, too. Serve at once. Serves 4 as a main dish or 8 as a side dish.

SAUCES FOR PASTA

VARYING SAUCES make daily pasta an adventure, not a sentence. I must admit, though, that were we to take a poll, I'm sure our family favorite would remain our tried-and-true meat sauce, hands down. Especially if it's made with home-grown and home-packed tomatoes. One of the main reasons Italians seldom eat at Italian restaurants is that they can get such better pasta and sauce at home! Any of these will dress one pound of pasta nicely.

Aglio e Olio Sauce

(GARLIC AND OIL)

This adds a beautiful shimmer to any dish of pasta.

1 cup Italian olive oil
8 cloves garlic, peeled and thinly sliced
1 cup water
1½ tablespoons finely chopped fresh parsley
½ teaspoon oregano
½ teaspoon freshly grated black pepper
1 teaspoon salt

In a saucepan, sauté the garlic in the oil over moderate heat until the garlic is golden brown. Add water and simmer for five minutes, stirring once or twice. Add parsley and seasonings and simmer uncovered another 10 minutes. Combine thoroughly with pasta before serving.

Tuna Sauce

To one recipe of Aglio e Olio (above) add one 7-ounce can tuna, flaked. Serve as above.

Anchovy Sauce

An uncooked sauce. The heat of the cooked pasta is sufficient to warm these ingredients; just be sure the anchovies are diced very fine.

¾ cup olive oil
2-ounce tin anchovy fillets, diced
⅓ cup fresh parsley, chopped fine
¼ cup lemon juice (from fresh lemon, not bottled)
½ teaspoon freshly grated black pepper

Combine all ingredients in a small mixing bowl and toss with hot pasta.

White Clam Sauce

This is especially nice with green pasta.

½ cup olive oil
2 cloves garlic, minced
¾ cup water
2 teaspoons finely chopped fresh parsley
½ teaspoon oregano
¾ teaspoon salt
½ teaspoon finely grated black pepper
1½ cups cherrystone clams and their juice

In a saucepan, sauté minced garlic in oil over moderate heat until garlic is lightly browned. Add water and stir until well combined. Add herbs and seasonings, clams and clam juice. Bring just to boiling point (any further cooking will toughen clams). Serve hot.

Ricotta Sauce

An exceedingly nutritious sauce, and very quick.

1 pound ricotta cheese
¾ cup water (approximately)
1 teaspoon salt
½ teaspoon freshly grated black pepper

In a saucepan, add water gradually to ricotta until desired consistency is reached. The exact amount needed will depend on the moisture content of the ricotta. The sauce should coat the pasta. Add seasonings and warm over medium heat for two minutes, taking care not to bring it to a boil. Serve hot.

White Sauce, Two Ways

These are the ones many children prefer to the more highly seasoned sauces.

White Sauce #1

3 tablespoons butter
2 egg yolks, beaten
1 cup grated Romano cheese
⅔ cup cream or sour cream
½ teaspoon freshly grated black pepper

In a saucepan, melt butter over low heat. Remove from heat and mix in egg yolks, cheese and cream. Add pepper and warm over low heat just to the boiling point. Stir a few times while warming. Excellent over ravioli.

White Sauce #2

1 tablespoon butter
4 ounces cream cheese
⅔ cup plain yogurt
1 cup grated Romano cheese
½ teaspoon grated black pepper

In saucepan, melt butter and cream cheese over low heat. Add yogurt, Romano cheese and pepper. Stir until well combined and just at the boiling point.

Tomato Sauce

Mom calls this "quick sauce" because it's not one that simmers for hours on the stove. That's Meat Sauce (next). "Quick sauce" is okay for an everyday lunch, but Meat Sauce is what you make for Sunday. Meat Sauce is what's being referred to around home when just the word sauce is used. This sauce has its own virtues, in my opinion, particularly the fresh taste of the tomatoes, which sings out more clearly here than in Meat Sauce. Also, the addition of just one extra ingredient can change the entire character of this one, allowing for quite a bit of experimentation.

1 clove garlic
¼ cup Italian olive oil
1 6-ounce can tomato paste
1 cup water
4 cups canned plum tomatoes, *or* 4 cups *very ripe* plum tomatoes (vine-ripened, with very thin skins and lots of juice)
2 or 3 bay leaves

In large saucepan, brown the garlic in olive oil over medium heat. Discard the garlic. Stir tomato paste into the flavored oil and keep stirring until it absorbs all the oil and browns slightly. Add water and stir until mixture is of even consistency. Add tomatoes and bay leaves. Simmer uncovered until the sauce thickens and the tomatoes have all but disintegrated. To hasten this process, press them with a fork or the back of your stirring spoon several times as they simmer. The sauce should be ready in a half to three quarters of an hour, depending on how juicy the tomatoes are. Yes, it does spatter about, but sauces cooked covered definitely taste less full-bodied. Makes one quart. Serve hot, garnished with grated Romano cheese.

Variations we use a lot:

With Frizzle

To basic recipe, add 3 pieces of pancetta (rendered pork rind, called *frizzle* in Pugliese dialect) when you add the tomato paste. Remove before serving.

With Hot Peppers

To basic recipe, add 1 or 2 small hot peppers, cleaned, but not cut up, when you add the tomatoes. Remove before serving.

With Mushrooms

To basic recipe, add ¾ cup thin-sliced, fresh mushrooms as you sauté the garlic in oil. These stay in.

Meat Sauce

In Grandma's time Thursdays and Sundays were sauce days. I have a friend trained at the Swiss hotel school in Lausanne who tasted some of this sauce when he was 19. He visited us last spring, 17 years later, with work all over Europe behind him (including a year in Florence), and he says this is still the best pasta sauce he ever tasted! We think so, too. This is the taste of home, the taste people look forward to enjoying with their reunion spaghetti. Made with different meats, the sauce takes on other flavors, but each is just as good as the next.

> 1 recipe Sunday Meatballs (see p. 105) *or*
> 1 recipe Braciole (see p. 107) *or*
> 1½ pounds Italian sweet or hot sausage (see p. 119)
>   *or*
> 1½ pounds veal, cut in 1″ cubes *or*
> ¾ pound beef and ¾ pound pork loin, in 1″ cubes *or*
> 2 pounds chicken parts, bones in *or*
> 6 pork chops
> Olive oil (enough to reach halfway up sides of meat)
> 1½ teaspoons oregano
> 1 double recipe Tomato Sauce (see p. 53)

In large skillet, brown the meat you've selected in oil until it is thoroughly cooked and crisp on the outside. Remove meat, reserving oil to brown the tomato paste. Drain on paper towels.

In a large kettle, place ingredients for Tomato Sauce, using the oil and meat drippings to brown the tomato paste. Add oregano. When sauce is ready to simmer, add browned meat. Bring to boiling point over medium heat, then reduce heat and simmer uncovered for 2 to 3 hours, or until meat is very tender or about to drop from its bones. Remove the meat to a separate serving dish. Combine sauce with pasta and serve from large platter or bowl with lots of grated Romano over all. Serves 8.

Marinara Sauce

Back when religious observances dictated abstention from meat for nearly a third of the year (Advent, Lent, the vigils of other Holy Days), this sauce appeared a great deal. A small amount of seafood added to the sauce goes a long way, an advantage with the cost of seafood what it is today. The onions add to this sauce the sweetness that comes from the meat in regular sauce. When seafood is used in sauce, the cooking time after it is added is much shorter than for a meat sauce. The seafood goes in only for the last half hour at the most.

        2 medium onions, chopped fine
        ¼ cup olive oil
        2 cloves garlic, minced
        1 teaspoon chopped basil
        4 cups plum tomatoes, canned or *very ripe* fresh with
                the thinnest of skins and lots of juice
        2 dozen clams in the shell, ready to cook (see p. 24)
                or
        1 dozen shucked oysters and their juice *or*
        ½ pound lobster or crab meat *or*
        2 dozen mussels in the shell, well-scrubbed *or*
        1 anchovy *or*
        1 salt-packed sardine *or*
        ½ pound small fresh shrimp, cleaned

In a large kettle, sauté the onions in the olive oil over medium heat until they are soft, golden and transparent. Add the garlic and cook over low heat, stirring occasionally, for 10 more minutes. Add the basil and tomatoes, pressing the tomatoes into chunks so they will give up their juice and blend into the sauce. Simmer uncovered for two hours, stirring every 15 to 20 minutes. Add your choice of seafood. If in a shell, cook only until shells are open wide. Otherwise, another 20 or 30 minutes is sufficient. With shrimp, add only for the last 3 or 4 minutes of cooking or they will become very tough. Arrange shells around edge of platter or serving bowl, or place directly on individual plates. Serve sauce hot, mixed well with pasta. Serves 4.

Spaghettini, Two Ways

Some people are very partial to spaghettini, very thin spaghetti, because of its light texture. Frank Argento and Aunt Esther agree that it's best with a very light sauce, but Aunt Esther adds another touch—seasoned bread crumbs. Both recipes make enough sauce for one pound spaghettini, cooked (see directions, p. 49).

#1—Frank Argento's Way

2 cloves garlic
1 cup olive oil
½ teaspoon freshly grated black pepper
2 ounces anchovies, cut in thin strips

In skillet, sauté garlic in oil until brown, then discard garlic. Add pepper, then anchovies. Stir until anchovies are well-coated with the flavored oil. Spoon mixture over spaghettini and toss gently until all strands of the pasta are coated with the sauce.

#2—Aunt Esther's Way

1 clove garlic
1 cup olive oil
½ cup water
2 ounces anchovies, cut in thin strips
1 tablespoon oregano
1 tablespoon minced parsley
½ cup toasted bread crumbs, preferably from day-old
   homemade Italian Bread (see p. 65)

In skillet, brown garlic in olive oil, then discard garlic. Stir in water, then anchovies. In mixing bowl, combine oregano, parsley and bread crumbs. Spoon oil mixture over pasta, tossing until well-coated. Garnish with crumb mixture.

Pasta with Peas

Grandpa insisted on it: lunch on the dot of noon. And throughout the summer when Grandma had to feed numerous extra people (visiting grandchildren and hired hands helping with strawberries and tomatoes), it was often this simple dish that she fixed.

The peas came directly from Grandma's garden, picked about mid-morning by us kids. Since there is probably nothing sweeter than the taste of raw, fresh-picked peas, only about half the peas we picked ever made it into the big earthenware bowl to be carried in to Grandma.

The pasta, little matchsticks, are hard to find ready made today, but regular spaghetti broken into 2-inch pieces achieves the same effect.

There were two shifts at the table, kids first while the men cleaned up and put their shirts back on, then ten or so grownups crowded around, bronzed from the sun and all talking at once. Of course, everyone was ravenous from working since 7:00, and this delicious aroma wafting from the kitchen sharpened appetites even more. The result: plates and plates of pasta and peas being consumed at a single sitting.

1 medium onion, chopped
⅓ cup olive oil
2 cups shelled fresh peas (frozen may be substituted,
    if necessary)
4 cups water, at full rolling boil
1 pound spaghetti, broken into 2″ pieces, cooked
    (see p. 49)
Salt and black pepper, freshly ground, to taste

In a small skillet, sauté onion in oil until onion is soft, golden and transparent. While the onion is cooking, put peas into saucepan with boiling water and cook, covered, for five minutes. Add onions and oil to peas and water, stirring to blend liquids. Cover and simmer on very low heat for half an hour. The onion flavor will permeate the peas. Salt and pepper to taste. Place cooked pasta into a large serving dish. Pour peas and cooking liquid over and toss lightly. Serve hot with grated Romano cheese. Serves 4.

PIZZA

*T*HERE ARE two basic kinds of pizza, one with a thin crust made with olive oil, the other with a thick crust made from regular bread dough (no olive oil). Neither, when made at home, bears the slightest resemblance to what's called pizza in most restaurants or pizzerias. That product, whatever it is, typically features a crust as thin as a dime that tastes like mushy cardboard and a sauce that's right out of a can, topped with an Americanism, "pizza cheese" (it melts like mozzarella, but doesn't have the flavor), and possibly strewn with a few gratuitous pieces of raw mushroom or preservative-laden sausage. No wonder it's categorized as "junk food"! No wonder people who care about food look askance at me when I declare that my favorite food is pizza! What I'm talking about is this, piping hot from my mother's oven, a complete meal in itself.

Elsie's Pizza Dough

> 4 cups unbleached flour
> 1½ level teaspoons salt
> 1 yeast cake, or 1 package dry yeast, dissolved in ¼
>   cup warm water
> 2 tablespoons olive oil
> 1 cup lukewarm water (approximately)
> Olive oil

In a large mixing bowl, combine flour and salt. Make a well in the center and add dissolved yeast and oil. Stir until flour becomes crumbly, then add water gradually, using only enough to allow the dough to come away from the sides of the bowl and form a moist, but not sticky, ball.

Flour your hands and your work surface, then turn out dough ball and knead 4 or 5 minutes until it becomes somewhat smoother and more elastic. Lightly coat the inside of the mixing bowl with oil and place dough in, then turn the ball over so the top surface is protected from drying by a thin film of oil. Cover the bowl with a damp cloth and let dough rise until doubled in bulk (about two hours). This makes enough dough for two pizza crusts.

While the dough is rising, make the sauce.

Elsie's Pizza Sauce

½ pound Italian Sweet Sausage, preferably
    homemade (see p. 118)
1 large onion, chopped
1 clove garlic, peeled
¼ cup olive oil
1 2-pound can concentrated Italian plum tomatoes or
    puree
1 6-ounce can tomato paste
1 cup thinly sliced mushrooms (fresh, if possible)
1 tablespoon finely chopped parsley
2 bay leaves

Remove casing from sausage and brown the meat in a skillet with onion and garlic in olive oil over medium heat. Discard garlic. Transfer meat mixture with a slotted spoon to a large kettle, reserving as much oil and drippings as possible for browning tomato paste. Add tomatoes or puree to meat mixture and bring to a simmer over medium heat. Add tomato paste and mushrooms to oil and drippings in skillet and brown over medium heat (the paste should absorb all the oil). Add paste and mushrooms to tomato mixture and stir to combine all ingredients. Add parsley and bay leaves, then simmer uncovered for two hours over low heat. Stir every 15 to 20 minutes. Makes 6 cups.

Pizza Toppings

For one pizza:

Olive oil
Pizza Sauce
8 ounces mozzarella cheese, roughly grated
½ cup grated Romano cheese
Salt and pepper
½ stick pepperoni, cut in thin rounds (optional) *or*
2 ounces anchovies, cut in thin strips (optional)

One may also add thin slices of pepper, thin slices of onion, thin strips of salami or prosciutto, capers, olives, baby shrimp, extra slivers of garlic, or the tiniest of meat balls (already cooked). Our favorite, though, is just Mom's sauce with mozzarella and Romano over the top. Of course, it already has sausage and onions and mushrooms as part of the sauce.

To assemble the pizza, punch dough down after it has finished rising and roll it out on a floured surface to the size and shape of your pizza pan (some round, some oblong). Roll the dough about ½-inch thick. Coat the pizza pan liberally with olive oil and arrange dough in the pan so the crust is of even thickness and there's a small roll around the edge to make it easier to hold while eating. Cover the dough with a layer of sauce, enough so you can't see the dough, but not so thick that it reaches the height of the roll around the edge. Too little sauce will mean a dry pizza; too much and the sauce will run all over when you try to serve it. Next, scatter the cheese uniformly over the sauce. Finally, add whatever else you want to put on it. Drizzle a little olive oil over all. Salt and pepper liberally. Bake *in the bottom* of a 400° oven for 25 to 30 minutes, or until crust is golden brown and the cheese is bubbling. If you put the pizza on the top rack, the cheese will brown and harden long before the crust is done. Cut in individual pieces (we use scissors) and serve hot.

Pizza Fritte

This is what you do with any leftover pizza dough. In our house, I always make sure to have some left over because the kids like this the next morning for breakfast, as Italian children always have.

Pizza dough
Olive oil (enough to stand ½-inch deep in your
    skillet)
Powdered sugar, honey or jam

On a floured surface, roll out small pieces of dough quite thin, to a width of about 3 inches.

Heat oil over medium high heat in skillet. Drop in dough rounds, turning when first side is golden brown. Dough will puff dramatically as it cooks. Remove as soon as second side is golden brown, using tongs or slotted pancake turner. Drain on paper towels.

Serve hot with a dusting of powdered sugar, a drizzle of honey or a dollop of jam.

BREAD

G*RANDMA'S BREAD* was like no other: it stood tall in a solid chunk, golden sides and top, with the thinnest of crusts and a fine-grained, creamy-colored inside. Warm out of the oven it smelled yeasty and toasty, begging for a layer of melting, freshly-churned butter to make it completely irresistible. Slicing the loaf was a feat strictly reserved for grownups. The bread knife was far too massive for a child's hands and the peasant style of wielding it (grasping the loaf close to one's chest with the left hand while drawing the blade through the entire thickness in one fierce sweep, barely managing not to slit one's throat) scared me to death. The virtue in this method is that thick slices result, the reason Grandma's sandwiches could hold their own with the most zesty fillings. Grandpa always stood at the head of the table to slice bread, the official start of the meal.

Grandma made bread 12 loaves at a time from wheat grown on the farm and milled in nearby Vernon. Unbleached and fresh, the flour was stored under the attic staircase (the coolest spot in the house) in a hip-high golden metal bin. To mix the dough, Grandma used a large wooden tub that she used for nothing else. And, of course, all the dough was worked on her bread board. The fineness of the grain was due to the four risings (three in the big tub and one in the pans). All these factors contributed to the heft, the sweet smell, the satisfying texture and the crisp crust that put commercial breads to shame.

Italian Bread

2 fresh yeast cakes (should be moist, pearly gray,
     with no black spots)
½ cup warm water
5 pounds unbleached flour (approximately 20 cups)
¼ cup salt
4 cups or more warm water
Flour
1 cup melted butter

Dissolve yeast cakes in warm water (about body temperature).

In a very large pan (a turkey roaster works well) combine flour and salt. Add yeast dissolved in water, then two cups more water. Stir mixture with a heavy spoon at first, then as you gradually add more water, use both hands to turn the mass around and around until all is thoroughly mixed and quite sticky. Cover the pan with damp towels and place in a warm spot to rise (an oven with a pilot light is ideal as there are no cool drafts; however, the dough will rise, no matter where you put it, even in the refrigerator—the cooler the spot, the longer the rising takes). When the dough has doubled in bulk, punch it down with your fist and divide into six pieces. Knead each piece on a well-floured surface for five minutes. Return all pieces of dough to pan for a second rising, covering again with damp towels. Repeat kneading and return to pan for third rising.

Punch dough down for the last time and shape into round loaves that can be baked on liberally greased cookie sheets or pizza pans or into oblongs that touch all sides of liberally greased bread pans (5″ × 9″). Let rise for a fourth time until dough reaches the tops of the pans and tops are rounded. If making round loaves, they should double in volume. Just before putting in the oven, slash the top with a very sharp knife and drizzle in melted butter or brush melted butter over the top. Bake on the bottom rack of a 375° oven for 45 minutes. Check to see if sides have retracted from sides of the pan and that top and bottom are golden brown. The loaf should drop easily from the pan and sound hollow when tapped. If the bottom seems whitish, bake 5 or 10 minutes more or until loaf tests done.

Cool bread to room temperature, turned upside down on racks, before wrapping in foil or plastic bags. At Grandma's storage was never a problem: the bread would disappear long before it spoiled! Makes 6 loaves.

Onion Bread

A fragrant variation of plain bread that's good with melted cheese for a quick lunch or snack.

    3 cups onions, chopped fine
    ⅓ cup olive oil
    3 loaves bread, risen in baking pans

In medium-sized skillet, sauté onions in oil over medium heat until they are transparent. Transfer to small bowl with a slotted spoon, draining off as much of the oil as possible.

When loaves are halfway through their baking time, spoon onions over the top of each loaf. They will brown as the loaf completes the baking time. Makes 3 loaves.

Sausage Bread

One of Aunt Esther's most popular innovations. This, some fresh, raw vegetables on a relish tray, and a few glasses of wine make a wonderful picnic lunch, too.

⅓ recipe Italian Bread dough (see p. 65), risen once
2 cups onions, chopped
½ cup olive oil
1 pound sweet Italian sausage, casings removed
2 eggs, slightly beaten
1 cup coarsely grated mozzarella cheese
½ cup grated Romano cheese
1 teaspoon garlic powder
Salt and pepper to taste
Olive oil

Punch down dough and divide into two pieces. Let rest while you prepare the filling.

In a large skillet, sauté the onions until soft in olive oil. In another skillet, cook sausage until browned and crumbly, stirring occasionally to prevent the meat from clumping. Drain off the drippings and place cooked sausage in large mixing bowl with cooked onions and olive oil. Add eggs, cheeses, garlic powder, salt and pepper. Mix well.

Roll out one of the dough pieces on a floured surface into an oblong approximately ½-inch thick. Spread half the filling mixture evenly over the top of the dough. Roll up like a jellyroll, starting with the longer side of the dough so the finished loaf is longer than it is in diameter. Otherwise, the loaf may not cook through. To prevent the filling from leaking out, pinch the ends of the dough together. Repeat with second dough piece and the rest of the filling mixture.

Lift loaves into greased bread loaf pans (5″ × 9″) and brush tops with a thin film of olive oil. Let rise for one hour, or until pans are full and tops are rounded. Bake at 400° for 30 to 35 minutes. Cool to room temperature before slicing. Makes 2 loaves.

Thick Pizza (Faggats)

Why this is called *faggats* (accent on last syllable) in Pugliese dialect, nobody seems to know, but one or another of my father's cousins can be counted on to bring a pan of it to the reunion every year. It's the dish that comes instantly to mind whenever talk turns to "the feast," family shorthand for the Feast of Saints Cosma and Damiano (September 27). Though we weren't an obsessively religious family, Grandma never missed the devotions honoring the "saintly physicians." It was a feast that had originated back home in Alberobello and one our people established in Utica as soon as they arrived. At first 200 to 300 *paesani* organized a shrine to the saints; then, from 1915 on, solemn Masses were offered at St. Anthony's Church for the thousands of pilgrims who began making their way to Utica from all over the East Coast and Canada.

Why a particular group of people latches onto a particular saint for veneration over hundreds of years makes interesting sociological and anthropological speculation. But in the case of Saints Cosma and Damiano, it's not hard to understand their popularity: they were physicians, dedicated to Christ, who refused payment for their services! As the patron saints of physicians, Saints Cosma and Damiano are invoked by the faithful when illness strikes. My grandmother believed in them absolutely, as do millions of others around the world who

continue to attribute miraculous cures to the saints' interces-
sion. As a child, I must admit, the religious significance of the
feast was way over my head. What impressed me were the
procession and the street festival that went on for three or four
days—a kaleidoscope of lights, color, motion and booth after
booth piled high with Italian delicacies.

Our view of the procession was one of the best: we could
see for blocks from the porch of our third-story flat on
Elizabeth Street. This was in the days before Macy's Thanksgiving Day parade and the Tournament of Roses parade were
broadcast in living color to all parts of the country.

My sisters and I watched in high spirits as the members of
the men's societies at church solemnly turned the corner onto
our street. They were followed by the Cross, carried by
acolytes and accompanied by clergy, altarboys, and little
flower girls wearing their First Communion dresses and veils.
Next came the women of the church carrying hand-embroi-
dered banners of their societies; the heavy statues of Saints
Cosma and Damiano mounted on carts being pushed by men
who felt honored to be asked to do this work; the Fort
Schuyler Band (La Banda Rosa) whose shiny brass carried
Italian festival music to every home along the route; the Italian
and American flags; members of religious societies from other
churches and other cities; and for block after block, streams of
pilgrims, many aged and wearing black, carrying lighted votive
candles and saying the Rosary. Every so often the carts
carrying the statues would stop, allowing spectators to run up
and pin money offerings to the brilliant red satin ribbons
draped around the figures of the saints. The procession was a
perfect blend of the religious and the worldly, both a genuine
expression of piety and a rousing good time.

For me, the biggest thrill of all was being allowed to stay out
past dark on the nights of the feast, even when there was
school the next day. My mother gave me a quarter to spend
each night, most of which I would spend on thick pizza. My
girlfriends usually preferred buying cotton candy, tortoni, or

the kewpie dolls on sticks we all thought were the most beautiful playthings imaginable. We would wander down the entire length of stalls at the street festival, the sausage sizzling, the sauce bubbling, the meat on skewers roasting, the peppers frying, carefully considering each possibility, but I always wound up at the thick pizza stand, ready to surrender my precious quarter, too timid to request it, but hoping to get a corner piece (extra crunchy). This dish remains exotic for me, redolent with someone else's spicy sauce and sweet onions— a symbol of what it means to be 10 years old and just beginning to get a glimpse of what the grownup world is like.

> Olive oil
> ⅓ recipe Italian bread dough (see p. 65), risen once
> 3 cups *very ripe* plum tomatoes, fresh or canned
> 1 6-ounce can tomato paste
> 3 large onions, chopped fine
> ½ cup olive oil
> 1 cup oil-cured black olives, with pits removed
> Salt and black pepper, freshly ground

Generously coat the bottom and sides of a 12 inch × 17 inch baking or roasting pan with olive oil. On a lightly floured surface, roll out the dough to a thickness of 1 inch and shape it to fit the bottom of the pan. Transfer the dough into the pan, cover with damp towels, and allow to rise ¾ of the way up the sides of the pan. While it rises, prepare the topping.

Slice tomatoes and discard as many seeds as possible. In a large saucepan, bring tomatoes to boil over medium heat, then reduce heat, stir in tomato paste, and simmer uncovered until somewhat thickened (about 45 minutes).

In a skillet, sauté onions, covered, in ½ cup olive oil until they are transparent and soft.

Cut olives into halves.

To assemble pizza, spoon tomatoes over top of risen dough, spreading them evenly and gently so as not to cause the dough to fall. Scatter onions and oil on top of tomatoes, then stud entire surface with olive halves. Salt and pepper lightly.

Bake in the middle of the oven at 350° for 30 minutes or until tips of onions start to brown and the undercrust is golden brown. Cut with bread knife into squares after pizza has cooled a bit, but is still warm. Trying to cut it just after it comes from the oven will shred the pieces and make the edges clump together. Makes 15 pieces.

Barese Onion Pizza

This is something like *faggats* with a top, but made with rolled out pizza dough instead of risen bread dough. Mr. Joseph Granieri and Mrs. Beatrice Durante DeSantis, whose families ran grocery stores in East Utica and were friends of my grandparents, recalled this recipe for me the afternoon I was accepted into the Società Pugliese. Founded in 1911 as a mutual aid society for people from Apulia, the organization today awards prizes for excellence in Italian language studies, plans social events and marks the births, marriages, illnesses and deaths of member families. Some might look on such societies as anachronisms, but I think they serve an important function: reminding us of our personal heritage in an increasingly anonymous world. I was very proud to be voted in in the traditional way—people stand up to be counted—in the presence of people whose family names have been linked with ours since before my father was born.

The day I became a member, the main topic for discussion was the upcoming annual picnic. Back in the 1920s when over 500 people would get together for the food, the music, the dancing and the raffle (in 1927, a new car!), a dish such as this would be a highlight of the menu—a real taste of the Old Country.

2 cups chopped sweet onions or scallions
⅓ cup olive oil
1½ cups *very ripe* plum tomatoes (or well-drained canned ones)
¼ pound oil-cured black olives, pits removed
Salt and black pepper, freshly grated
1 recipe pizza dough (see p. 60)
Olive oil

In a large skillet, sauté onions or scallions in olive oil over moderate heat until they are soft, golden and transparent. Cut up tomatoes and stir in. Simmer for 15 minutes on low heat. Remove from heat. Cut pitted olives in halves and combine with tomato mixture. Season with salt and pepper.

Divide pizza dough into two parts. Roll out one half on a floured surface to a thickness of one inch and in an oblong shape large enough to fill a 9 inch × 13 inch baking pan with an inch overhang all around. Coat baking pan liberally with olive oil, then fit in dough. Spread filling mixture evenly over crust. Roll out second half of dough to form a top crust. Place over filling, then roll up overhanging dough from undercrust to form a decorative edge, sealing top and bottom crusts together. Slit the top crust with a sharp knife in four or five places or prick top all over with a fork to allow steam to escape during baking. Bake for 30 minutes in the middle of a 350° oven, or until top and bottom crusts are golden brown. Makes 12 pieces.

Simmering conserva
and polishing tomatoes for market

4

Vegetables

VEGETABLES, WHICH many people feel they could just as soon do without (and when they're boiled limp, we agree), add conspicuous joys to our reunion meal. They reach the table displaying their versatility: as antipasti, in pasta dishes and sauces, and as side dishes *(contorni)* presented with meat, poultry, or seafood main dishes. First choice, naturally, are the fresh vegetables in season at the time of the reunion. By fresh my parents mean picked no more than an hour or two before they are to be served. In fact, my father's directions for doing corn on the cob start, "Go pick some corn. . . !" In Central New York in summertime this is not hard to accomplish since roadside stands with fresh corn dot the landscape, and it's even possible to phone in an order to be picked just before you arrive.

In keeping with general Italian preference, we like vegetables picked just as they mature, even on the small side. Plum tomatoes with pinkish tops and firm bodies, therefore, are better for salad than the reddest, ripest, juiciest ones. By the same token, baby eggplants are considered superior to larger ones which usually have developed a quite seedy pulp. With squash, zucchini, and pumpkin, we don't even wait until the fruit makes an appearance: the blossoms are picked, breaded, and fried, an amazingly light and delicate dish. My father believes this is one way to identify an Italian restaurant where you might be able to get a decent meal—ask if they make *fiori di zucca (cocozza,* in Pugliese) in season. If nobody ever heard of it, they're probably too far removed from the garden to know much about good food!

Over the winter Grandma relied on what she'd put up over the summer and fall. From July on the cellar started filling up with jars and jars of pickles, peppers, peas, green beans, corn, mushrooms, onions, eggplant, and tomatoes, tomatoes, tomatoes—some in the form of paste *(conserva).* Popcorn on the cob hung, drying, from the rafters. Squash, onions and potatoes wintered in bushel baskets (the cellar stays at 45° to 50° with just the right amount of moisture to keep these in good condition) while carrots and cabbages would be left outside on the ground with a cover of leaves or straw. These days, Mom freezes a good deal of the farm produce, but after each visit home we return with our station wagon filled with jars of fruits, jams, juices, and tomatoes, tomatoes, tomatoes—doing our part to relieve the strain on those old wooden cellar shelves!

For my own family, I make a Thursday visit to Al and Nick's grocery in Ossining, the next village downriver from ours. There I'm sure to find whatever Italian specialties are in season and I have the pleasure of choosing from produce that seems days fresher than what's in the supermarkets. The men who work there remind me a lot of the *paesani* who hung around with my grandfather, and we sometimes strike up a conversation. One week I didn't shop on Thursday and came in the next Monday instead. The remaining plum tomatoes were in a remarkably ripe condition, their thin skins barely able to contain the heavy pulp. The proprietor offered them to me for half price; then, unsure whether I'd be old enough to understand what he was talking about, I guess, he explained,

"They're still good for sauce." He beamed when I enthusi-
astically agreed, telling him I always make sauce from scratch.
I could tell I'd struck a responsive chord when he launched
into a discussion of today's food preparation standards. "It's a
crime," he said, "but very few people do this anymore."
Then, with deep conviction, "That's the most important thing
you can do for your family, you know, feed them right." I
nodded my head and took all the plum tomatoes.

I think he's recognized a fellow spirit. Now, whenever I go
in with the children, I always find an extra tangerine, apple or
orange for each of them tucked into our order box. The sauce
made from those tomatoes that day, by the way, was the best
of the whole year:

TOMATOES

*O*UR FAMILY life would not have been the same without
tomatoes. None for salad, none for sauce, none for soup—a
diminished existence. Between the tomatoes and the
strawberries, both crops that demand a high degree of hand
tending, it's a wonder there was any time left for corn, beans
and peas; but somehow everything got done and the crops
made it to market.

Grandpa followed a simple rule about when to sow tomato
seed—every Saint Joseph's Day, March 19. For about a week
before, he'd go to work in the big greenhouse, stoking up the
pot-bellied stove to warm the soil in the hundreds of flats, then
meticulously sifting the soil and grooming the surface to
receive the fine tomato seed. He saved seed from year to year
(Early Ann, Bonny Best, Valiant), starting early- and late-
maturing varieties together to insure steady production over
many weeks' time come summer. Just three smallish linen

bags (each fit easily in my grandfather's hand) held enough seed to yield 12,000 seedlings (plus another hundred for the family garden) ready to be set out eight weeks later.

We children had little to do with the plants out in the field, but every tomato that left Grandpa's for market was hand-polished—and that's where everybody in the family got back into the picture. Summer Sunday afternoons would see us grouped under the maples or out by the fireplace, carefully rubbing the surface of each tomato with soft cotton cloths, exclaiming over the giants and holding them up for all to see. No picking of hard, green tomatoes here. Each was fully ripe, red and meaty—perfect, with no cracking of the skin—or it didn't make it onto the truck. Grandpa was a perfectionist, and it was a real sign of growing up to be allowed to participate in the tomato polishing. Handling the tomatoes, so heavy for their size, so pungent, so smooth, was a sensory delight—the full realization of possibilities we could only imagine in the greenhouse. Secretly, I think we were only too happy when Grandpa vetoed a particular piece: we got to eat it on the spot, often while it still held some of the sun's warmth.

Tomatoes with Basil

One step removed from eating them out of hand.

4 cups sliced fresh, ripe tomatoes
1 tablespoon minced fresh basil leaves
Salt and black pepper, freshly ground
3 tablespoons olive oil
1 tablespoon wine vinegar

Arrange the tomato slices in a shallow serving dish, trying to retain as much of their juice as possible. In a small mixing bowl, combine basil, salt, pepper, oil and vinegar. Pour over tomatoes. Juice from the tomatoes will mingle with the dressing. Set aside to allow flavors to blend, tilting the dish several times and spooning the liquid over the top of the tomatoes. Serve after 30 minutes to 4.

Tomato and Cucumber Salad

This was Grandpa's lunchtime favorite in summer when all ingredients were just picked.

3 cups plum tomatoes, barely ripe, cut in quarters
3 cups young cucumbers, cut in ½-inch slices
⅓ cup olive oil
3 tablespoons wine vinegar
Salt and black pepper, freshly ground

In a large salad bowl, gently mix tomatoes and cucumbers. Pour oil and vinegar over them, then salt and pepper to taste. Turn once or twice before serving to 6.

Tomato Sandwich

My father's favorite quick summer lunch. As in all things, the simplest is the best.

1 large, fully ripe tomato, preferably just off the vine
2 thick slices Italian bread, preferably homemade (see
    p. 65)
Mayonnaise

Slice the tomato into ¼-inch thick rounds. Spread mayonnaise liberally on both slices of bread. Arrange tomato slices evenly on one slice of bread and cover with the other. Serves one. If doing these for a crowd, place a tray of sliced tomatoes and a tray of sliced bread in the center of the table, pass the mayonnaise, and let everybody make their own.

Stuffed Tomatoes, My Way

Grandma would have considered this making a lot of extra fuss, but I like these served just slightly warm as part of a luncheon buffet. They go fast at the reunion because they complement fried chicken and fried fish so well. From a hostess's point of view, they win high marks because they require neither refrigeration nor heating at the last moment.

4 large, firm, ripe tomatoes
¾ cup very fine Italian bread crumbs
¼ cup grated Romano cheese
2 anchovy fillets, minced
2 tablespoons minced parsley
1 teaspoon lemon juice
⅓ cup olive oil (approximately)
Salt and black pepper, freshly ground
Black olives, pepper strips, onion strips (optional)

Cut off top quarter of each tomato and scoop out seeds and pulp (save the pulp to be added to a batch of sauce). Discard seeds. In a small mixing bowl, combine crumbs, cheese, anchovies, parsley, lemon juice and as much of the olive oil as needed to form a heavy stuffing. Spoon in the stuffing, filling tomatoes not quite to the brim. Sprinkle a bit of oil on top of the filling, then salt and pepper lightly. Decorate tops with halves of oil-cured black olives (pits removed) or very thin strips of sweet green pepper or onions, dipped in oil before being arranged on the tomatoes. Transfer tomatoes to a shallow baking pan and bake in the middle of the oven at 350° for an hour, or until tomatoes appear wrinkled and clinging to the filling. Cool to room temperature. Serves 4.

Mixed Summer Vegetables

A sort of ratatouille, but with garlic alone as a seasoning, rather than the French mixed herbs. My husband likes this with Italian bread just out of the oven to dip into the flavored oil after the vegetables are gone.

3 cups very ripe tomatoes, sliced and seeds removed
1 cup olive oil (approximately)
2 summer squash or 3 small zucchini, sliced ¼-inch
    thick
2 cups Italian sweet peppers (green bell peppers may
    be substituted), sliced into thin rounds
2 cups thinly sliced sweet onions
Salt and black pepper, freshly ground
1 clove garlic, minced

In a large skillet, sauté the tomatoes over medium heat in 3 tablespoons of the oil until tomatoes are warmed through and most of their juice has evaporated. Remove tomatoes from

pan and set aside in the bottom of a large serving dish while
you sauté each of the other ingredients individually, adding a
bit of fresh oil to the pan with each succeeding vegetable. Do
not allow the oil to heat to the point of smoking. The garlic
should be cooked only until it is golden brown, otherwise it
will add a bitter taste to the dish. As each vegetable is done,
add to the serving dish, making individual layers as you go.
Salt and pepper each layer lightly. Pour the minced garlic and
cooking oil over the top and serve warm or at room
temperature. Serves 4.

Canned Tomatoes, Grandma's Way

When, in August, we're blessed with an overabun-
dance of tomatoes from our few backyard plants, my thoughts
turn to Grandma and I am staggered with the knowledge that
she, almost singlehandedly, had to cope with the output of a
hundred plants! How it must have seemed, an inundation of
bushel after bushel, day after day, until I'm sure she must
have been seeing tomatoes in her sleep. But I don't remember
hearing any complaints—no muttering over the canner, no
railing at deities about her fate, no surreptitious cheering for
tomato bugs to stem the rolling red tide through her kitchen.
Just a steady work pace and a near-continuous cloud of steam
rising from the kettle on the rack of the side yard fireplace.
Grandma moved the canning operation there on sunny days
to have a cooler place to work and a better vantage point for
keeping track of the eight kids. She knew that daily pasta
required daily sauce, and it was up to her to provide them
both. What a knack for organization! What energy! What a
woman!

1 bushel ripe tomatoes (about 55 pounds)
Salt
Bay leaves
Water

Sterilize 18 one-quart glass canning jars by immersing them for 15 minutes in boiling water. Lift out with tongs. When handling subsequently, be sure not to touch the inside of the jars.

Wash each tomato carefully under running water to remove all traces of dust, spray (if you've grown them yourself, this shouldn't be a problem), and insects. Inspect each piece and make sure to discard any portions that seem overripe or discolored. Cut out and discard stem and core, but do not peel. Depending on size, cut into halves or quarters on a shallow tray that can hold the juice. Pack tomatoes rather tightly into a jar (but not so tight as to squash the fruit) along with two or three bay leaves. Fill to within ½ inch of the jar top. Add ¼ teaspoon salt, then reserved juice. Fill with boiling water to cover tomatoes. Follow manufacturer's instructions for sealing lids.

Place a rack in the bottom of a large, heavy pan or kettle (serious cooks invest in a home canner) and set sealed jars on the rack. Allow 2 inches of space between jars and the sides of the kettle. Fill the kettle with cool water to a depth of 1½ inch over the lids of the jars. Bring the water to a full boil over high heat and continue to boil another 30 minutes. Do not cover the kettle. Keep another pot of boiling water nearby to add more water when needed, as some evaporates in steam.

To remove jars from boiling water, use tongs to grasp them by their sides. Do not lift up by the lids as you may break the seal. Cool on a solid surface on a cushion of towels to prevent cool drafts from cracking the glass. Cool to room temperature; then, to keep color bright, store in a cool (50° to 60°) place. Makes approximately 18 quarts.

Tomato Paste (Conserva)

The watchword here is *pazienza* (patience). Slow, gentle simmering in a copper kettle over an outdoor wood fire made Grandma's *conserva* very sweet, not harsh like some commercial pastes. And, no, she never added sugar. She never added anything—just tomatoes.

To do this requires a stretch of several hours when you have planned *absolutely nothing else* because without frequent, thorough stirring the tomatoes will scorch and the paste will be bitter. To keep her hands from getting burned, Grandpa carved extra-long wooden spoons for Grandma to use while stirring. It's possible that their long contact with the tomatoes also added something to the taste of the finished product. In any case, this is an activity for a rainy day and at least two of your favorite opera recordings (the paste does well bubbling in time to the "Dove sono" of *The Marriage of Figaro*).

6 quarts ripe tomatoes, washed and sliced thin
(approximately 18 pounds)

Place tomatoes into large, heavy kettle and cook over medium heat until they are soft. Remove from heat and cool until you can handle them comfortably. Force through a strainer or food mill with holes small enough to trap the seeds. Discard seeds and skins. Return pulp to kettle and bring to simmer point. Reduce heat as low as possible, to just maintain the simmer. Stir every 5 to 10 minutes for several hours until paste reaches desired consistency. Spoon into sterilized pint glass canning jars. Follow manufacturer's instructions for sealing lids, then use canning and cooling procedure above (see p. 82). To use in making sauce, reconstitute with an equal amount of water. Makes approximately 6 pints.

Green Beans in Tomato Sauce

Here's one way all those tomatoes were used. When beans were in season, Grandma often substituted them for packaged pasta, thereby saving a bit on the cash outlay for food. This dish can also be made with canned or frozen green beans, but note the shorter cooking time required.

> 1 clove garlic, peeled
> ½ cup olive oil
> 2 medium onions, chopped
> 8 cups canned tomatoes, drained
> 2 bay leaves
> 6 cups green beans, preferably fresh
> 3 large potatoes, cut in 1-inch chunks

In a large saucepan, sauté the garlic in olive oil over moderate heat until garlic is browned. Discard garlic. Add onions to flavored oil and sauté until soft and golden. Stir in tomatoes and bay leaves and simmer, uncovered, until sauce thickens (about 45 minutes). Add fresh beans and simmer, covered, for another 45 minutes. Add potatoes to mixture after the beans have been in for 25 minutes. If you are using canned or frozen beans, add potatoes at the same time and cook only for another 20 minutes. Both beans and potatoes should absorb some of the sauce, but not dissolve in it. Pass grated Romano cheese and slices of homemade bread as accompaniments. Serves 4.

Corn-on-the-Cob

On reunion day, this is one of the biggest deals of all. I can't think of anyone who doesn't love corn-on-the-cob, especially when it's being prepared right at the edge of the cornfield! The prime enemy of really superb corn is overcooking: the natural sugar in the corn turns to starch, resulting in a dulled taste and a mushy texture. Properly cooked, fresh corn has full kernels with thin skins that burst easily when you bite into them, releasing milky sweet juices and the light heart of the kernel.

To select corn at the market, look for ears with pliable husks (not papery and dried out), even-sized, plump kernels (pull back the husk to get a good look), and no evidence of discoloration or soft spots. Varieties will differ in color, ranging from intense yellow to almost white, but kernels of any individual ear should be uniform in color unless, of course, it is a variegated variety. When you hold an ear in your hand it should feel full and solid, weighty for its size. The tassel of cornsilk should be brown and dry. Try to buy at a store where the corn is kept refrigerated (this retards the transformation of sugar to starch) and if you aren't going to cook it right away, refrigerate your purchase at home, too. Avoid pre-husked corn; it's likely to be dry and starchy without its protective cover.

We load the corn into Uncle Fred's steamer about a half hour before the main dishes are served. Some people steam corn in the husk, but we prefer to shuck it. When doing corn for a crowd like ours (about 12 dozen ears), make sure the steam is at full blast before loading the steamer, otherwise your cooking time will be longer and you'll have to keep checking to see if the corn is ready. Maintain a 2-inch depth of water in the bottom of the steamer throughout the process. Check at 20 minutes. If not ready, check again every two minutes until it suits your taste. Remove from steamer with tongs to save your fingers. Pile on large serving tray and let people help themselves. Pass salted butter and salt. An occasional person likes to grind on some fresh pepper too, but they are rare in our family. Break the ears in half to serve children.

A small amount of corn can be done on your stovetop either of two ways:

8 ears fresh corn-on-the-cob, shucked
Water

To steam, fill a large kettle with water to a depth of 2 inches. Bring to a full boil, covered, then insert steamer basket or colander into kettle. Place corn into basket and replace cover. Cook for 15 minutes after steam builds up.

Or, to boil, place ears of corn into kettle and fill with cool water until corn is covered. Remove ears and bring water to full, rolling boil. Add corn and cook 5 to 7 minutes after the water resumes a full boil. Serve as above to 4.

Mashed Broccoli

For all those who can't convince their children that broccoli are really little trees. I shunned broccoli for years until my mother came up with this way to fix it.

1 large head fresh broccoli, or two packages frozen
¼ cup butter
½ cup grated Romano cheese
½ cup Italian bread crumbs
¼ teaspoon garlic salt

Cut off the florets of the broccoli, then trim the large stem of any woody parts and cut into 1-inch-thick slices. Rinse under running water. Place the florets and stem pieces in a steamer basket or colander and fit inside a large saucepan with 2 inches of water in the bottom. Bring the water to boil and cover pan. Steam until broccoli is very tender, about 15 to 20 minutes. Alternatively, place florets and stem pieces in a saucepan with 2 inches of boiling water and boil covered 10 to 12 minutes. Drain.

Mash broccoli with fork or potato masher. Add butter and cheese, stirring until they are well combined with the broccoli. In a small bowl, mix bread crumbs and garlic salt. Transfer broccoli mixture to serving dish and garnish with seasoned crumbs. Serves 4.

Cardoon Patties

Cardoons are an artichoke substitute when the stalks are prepared with lemon, onion and butter and served with a sprinkling of grated cheese. These patties are served during Lent as a meat substitute. In both instances, cardoons help stretch a tight food budget and make interesting additions to routine fare. Obtain cardoons at an Italian grocery or grow your own. The May 1981 issue of *Attenzione* magazine has a beautifully illustrated article by Walter Chandoha about planting an Italian garden. Cardoons are included.

1½ pounds cardoon stalks
6 quarts water
Juice of two lemons
1¼ cups Italian bread crumbs
4 eggs, beaten
½ cup grated Romano cheese
1 clove garlic, minced
1½ teaspoons salt
Black pepper, freshly ground
Olive oil

Scrub cardoons under running water. Trim leaves and woody segments and discard. Cut stalks into pieces 3 to 4 inches long. In a large saucepan, bring three quarts of water to a boil and add juice of one lemon. Add cardoons and simmer for 10 minutes. Drain and rinse again under running water. This should remove bitterness. Draw another three quarts of water for pan. Bring to a boil and add juice of second lemon. Add cardoons and reduce heat. Simmer for 1½ hours, or until cardoons are very tender. Drain, then place cardoons in large mixing bowl.

Mash cardoons with fork, then add eggs, bread crumbs, cheese, garlic, salt and pepper. Stir thoroughly until mixture is of an even texture. Add as much olive oil as necessary to moisten the mixture so that you can form it into patties. Shape six hamburger-sized patties and fry until browned in olive oil in a large skillet. Serves 6.

Greens

Dandelion leaves, mustard greens, endive, escarole, turnip, kale, or collards: this recipe works well for all of them. Since they are all very bitter, the major portion of the cooking time is given to successive boilings and drainings—until they reach the degree of bitterness you find appetizing. The wonderful thing about these is that so many of them are free for the digging. Greens offer a counterpoint in flavor and texture to more highly seasoned foods, making them welcome side dishes on the reunion table.

2 pounds young, tender greens (pick before plant
   flowers)
¼ pound pancetta (frizzle) or salt-cured ham
½ cup olive oil
1 clove garlic, peeled and bruised
½ teaspoon salt
¼ cup grated Romano cheese (optional)

Wash greens carefully under running water. Trim any
discolored areas or tough stems and discard. Chop greens
and place in large saucepan, cover with water, bring to boil,
remove from heat, and drain. Repeat, bringing fresh water to
boil as many times as necessary to reduce bitterness. Before
bringing to boil a final time, add pancetta or ham. Reduce
heat and simmer until greens are tender and almost all the
cooking water has evaporated, approximately 20 to 25
minutes. Transfer to serving dish.

In a small mixing bowl, combine olive oil, garlic clove and
salt. Spoon onto cooked greens and mix well. Garnish with
grated Romano cheese, if you choose. Discard garlic clove
before serving. Serve slightly warm to 4.

Greens and Beans

Making a meal of your greens—another good Lenten
(or any other time) alternative to meat.

2 cups dried white kidney beans *or*
2 20-ounce cans cannellini beans and packing liquid
1 recipe cooked and seasoned greens (see p. 89)
Salt and black pepper, freshly ground

If using dried beans, soak overnight. Drain, rinse, and discard any broken or discolored beans. In a large saucepan, cover beans with water and bring to boiling point. Reduce heat and simmer, covered, until beans are tender. Drain, reserving ¾ cup of the cooking liquid.

Place cooked beans, the reserved liquid, and cooked greens in large saucepan, bring to simmer point, and simmer another half hour over very low heat. Salt and pepper to taste. Serves 4.

Barese Fava Beans (I Fava Battuto)

When my father was growing up, Fridays meant *i fava* so Thursdays meant all the kids gathered around the kitchen table after school to sort and clean the batch Grandma would cook. Grandma was serious about *i fava:* she bought them in 100-pound bags. It is safe to say that every one of my father's brothers and sisters loathed, hated, and detested fava beans in those days—except at the feast, where little bags of toasted and salted favas were sold as a snack food. Now, though, they all get a dreamy look in their eyes when *i fava* are mentioned because "doing *i fava*" has become a special event, something done only once or twice a year. At the Società Pugliese, it's the same story. Heads turn and people say "O-o-o-o-h" when one of the members lets it be known that a daughter or daughter-in-law or next door neighbor is "doing *i fava*" pretty soon, and they've been invited to have some. More than just a bowl of creamed beans, it's become something of a ritual meal, complete with prescribed side dishes—even an accepted recipe for serving the leftovers the next day!

4 cups dried fava beans, peeled and split
6 medium potatoes, diced
1 tablespoon salt
4 cloves garlic, peeled
1 cup olive oil
6 slices Italian bread, preferably homemade

Soak dried, split fava beans overnight in 8 cups of water. Drain, rinse, and discard any broken or discolored beans. In a large kettle, cover beans, potatoes, and salt with water. Bring to full boil, then reduce heat and simmer, covered, until beans are tender. You may need to add more water occasionally as beans absorb water while they cook. Drain and transfer beans and potatoes to a large mixing bowl.

In a skillet, sauté the garlic in the olive oil over moderate heat until the garlic is browned. Discard garlic.

Cut bread into 1-inch cubes and allow to air dry.

Mash the beans and potatoes in the mixing bowl, adding flavored oil gradually. When mixture thins, beat with egg beater or electric mixer on low setting. Continue adding oil until mixture is creamed like a thick pudding and of an even texture throughout. Stir in the bread cubes so they are evenly distributed. Serve warm in bowls to 8.

Side dishes everyone has come to expect: a double recipe of cooked greens (some people then mix the greens into the beans, but this is considered an aberration by others), and a large dish of fried hot peppers. The creamy color of the beans is very attractive next to the green of the greens and the red of the peppers—the ultimate in Italian patriotism, red, white and green!

To serve leftovers the next day for lunch, stir two cups sweet onions, fried until soft in olive oil, into reheated bean mixture.

Macaroni and Beans
(Pasta e Fagioli)

Another classic way with beans. Aunt Esther still grows her own cranberry beans, and they add extra visual appeal to this dish.

2 cups dried beans (cranberry, white kidney or ceci)
4 cups water
2 cloves garlic, peeled
½ cup olive oil
1 pound small shell macaroni, cooked and drained
Salt and black pepper, freshly ground
Parsley sprigs

In large saucepan, cover beans with 4 cups water and bring to boiling point. Reduce heat and simmer until beans are tender. Refrigerate overnight.

In a skillet, brown garlic in olive oil over medium heat. Discard garlic. Reheat cooked beans, stirring in flavored oil, and simmer, covered, for one hour over very low heat. If the amount of liquid seems scanty, add a bit more water. Combine cooked and seasoned beans with macaroni in a large serving bowl. Salt and pepper to taste. Garnish with parsley sprigs. Serve hot to 4.

Uncle Fred's Mushroom Stew

Gathering mushrooms, especially tree mushrooms, has been one of Uncle Fred's pastimes for years. These grow only on hardwood trees (there's a lot of elm in our woods) and look like clams arranged in tiers. *Go mushrooming only with an expert as many varieties are poisonous and, to the untrained eye, the differences aren't that obvious.* Tree mushrooms can be cooked very simply by slicing and frying with onions and sausage, but this stew, with or without the meat, uses them in a more original way. The hot peppers are Uncle Fred's signature. Great with ice-cold beer.

> 5 tablespoons olive oil
> 2 cloves garlic, peeled
> 4 cups fresh tree mushrooms (cultivated mushrooms
>   can be substituted)
> 1 6-ounce can tomato paste
> 1 cup water
> ½ teaspoon salt
> ½ cup chopped celery
> 2 hot peppers, sliced
> 1 onion, sliced
> 1 teaspoon chopped parsley
> 1½ pounds beef round, cubed, or stewing veal,
>   cubed, browned (optional)

In a large frying pan, brown the garlic in olive oil over moderate heat. Discard the garlic. In a large kettle, cover mushrooms with water and bring to boil. Reduce heat and simmer five minutes. Drain, squeezing excess water from mushrooms. Place mushrooms in frying pan with flavored oil and sauté over moderate heat until mushrooms are browned. Remove mushrooms and set aside.

Add the tomato paste to the remaining oil and cook 2 or 3

minutes until paste browns slightly and absorbs the oil. Add water and stir until paste is evenly diluted. Return mushrooms to pan and add remaining ingredients. Simmer, covered, over low heat one hour, adding water as necessary to keep sauce the proper consistency. Add beef or veal, already browned, for last hour of cooking, if you wish. Serve hot to 4.

Salt Potatoes

Children love to dig potatoes out of the hills in which they grow and are rewarded with the tiny ones to carry home from the field. It's hard to believe the amount of salt required to float these, but it's essential if each potato is to wind up with the correct amount of salt coating. The combination of thin, hard crust of salt and light, mealy inside makes it hard to stop eating these. Yes, yes, I've read all about salt causing high blood pressure and every other disease plaguing modern man, but I don't believe it. The *paesani* all ate these and lived into their eighties in the dignity of good health. Of course, they sat down to eat them after a hard day's work in the sun, so replacing their bodies' sodium with that in salt potatoes may have been a necessity, not a gourmet's whim.

> 3 pounds new potatoes, 1 to 2 inches in diameter
> 5 quarts water
> 2 26-ounce boxes salt (to float all the potatoes)
> Butter
> Parlsey

In a large kettle, bring water to boil. Add potatoes, then salt. Bring back to boiling point over high heat, then reduce heat and boil another 10 to 15 minutes. Potatoes are done when they can be split easily with a fork and are completely encrusted with salt. Drain and serve split in two with butter and parsley garnish. Serves 8.

Raw Fries

Like hashed browns, but without bacon drippings. A quick way to do potatoes—the thinner the slices, the faster they cook. If the potatoes you're using have thin skins, you needn't peel them, just scrub.

3 pounds potatoes, peeled
¾ cup olive oil
Salt and black pepper, freshly ground
4 eggs, scrambled (optional)
3 medium onions, sliced thin (optional)

Slice potatoes very thin. In a large skillet, heat oil and add potatoes. Cook on first side over moderate heat until brown and crusty. Do not stir, but lift potatoes occasionally with spatula to prevent sticking. Turn over in as large sections as possible. When second side is browned, transfer to serving platter. Salt and pepper liberally. Serves 4 as a side dish.

To make a main dish for lunch, scramble eggs with the potatoes. Onions may be sautéed with the potatoes in either version as another variation.

Baked Potato Gnocchi

I love to cook these for company. The overlapping rounds make a lovely casserole and the cheese makes this a high-quality protein dish.

 6 medium potatoes
 3 cups water
 8 tablespoons butter
 1 pound ricotta cheese
 2 eggs, slightly beaten
 ¼ teaspoon grated nutmeg
 ½ teaspoon salt
 1 cup grated Romano cheese
 ½ cup whole wheat flour

Peel potatoes and slice very thin. Bring water to boil in large saucepan. Add potatoes and cook until tender (8 to 10 minutes). Drain (save water for later use in making bread) and mash potatoes until all lumps disappear.

In another large saucepan, melt 4 tablespoons of butter. Stir in ricotta, eggs, nutmeg, salt and ¾ cup Romano cheese. Combine well. Add mashed potatoes and flour, stirring over medium heat until mixture thickens to the point that it can support a spoon upright (very stiff).

Butter a pizza pan or other shallow baking pan of similar size. Spoon mixture into it, smoothing to approximately ½-inch thick. Refrigerate 30 minutes, or until firm.

Butter a 2-quart casserole dish with low sides. Using a 2-inch biscuit cutter or a glass with a 2-inch diameter, press into the potato mixture, forming rounds. Arrange them, with edges slightly overlapping, in the casserole dish. Melt 4 tablespoons butter and pour over gnocchi. Sprinkle the remaining Romano cheese over the top.

Bake at 375° for 25 minutes, or until top is golden brown and crisp. Serve immediately to 6.

Squash Blossoms
(Fiori di Cocozza)

Any squash, zucchini, or pumpkin plant can provide the blossoms you need—all are delicately perfumed and delicious. Pumpkins are the most abundant producers and even if you have no space to grow pumpkins to maturity, starting some plants just to harvest the blossoms makes great culinary sense! Otherwise, ask your Italian grocer to get some for you in summer on special order.

> 2 dozen squash blossoms, with firm petals, preferably open
> 3 eggs, beaten slightly with 2 tablespoons water
> ¼ teaspoon salt
> ⅛ teaspoon nutmeg
> ½ cup very finely ground cracker crumbs
> Light oil, such as peanut, safflower or sunflower

Rinse flowers gently by dipping into bowl of cool water. Hold any closed blossoms open to make sure no insects are trapped inside.

In small mixing bowl, combine eggs, water, salt and nutmeg. Dip each bloom into the egg mixture, then into the cracker crumbs. Move at once into a skillet with at least 2 inches of oil heated to a high temperature. To test oil, drop a pinch of cracker crumbs into it. If it bubbles up madly, the heat is correct. Do not, however, heat to the point of smoking as this will burn the delicate blossoms. Don't put too many flowers in at once—it's easy to lose track of which needs to come out. The oil will cover the blossom completely, so there's no need to turn. After about a minute (no more), the blossom will be golden brown. Lift out with a slotted spoon or small strainer. Drain on paper towels and keep warm in the oven until all flowers are cooked. Serve at once. Makes 6 portions.

Zucchini Bread

After you've sautéed them, pickled them, stuffed them, and sliced them into salads, you can make them into this. It's so light and spicy, it's really more a cake than a bread.

3 eggs
2 cups sugar
1 cup corn oil
2 cups zucchini, diced
2 teaspoons vanilla extract
1 teaspoon baking soda
¼ teaspoon baking powder
2 teaspoons cinnamon
1 teaspoon salt
3 cups unbleached flour
1 cup raisins, *or,*
1 cup walnuts

In a large mixing bowl, beat eggs, sugar and oil until mixture is of even texture. Add zucchini and vanilla, stirring until well combined.

In a second bowl, sift baking soda, baking powder, cinnamon, salt and flour together. Then fold in raisins or walnuts, making sure each piece is coated with the dry mixture. Add dry mixture to zucchini mixture, combining well until batter is smooth.

Pour into greased or oiled bread loaf pan. Bake one hour and 20 minutes in the middle of the oven at 375°. Let loaf rest in pan 10 minutes before taking it out to complete cooling. Use a knife with a serrated edge to slice after loaf is at room temperature. Makes 1 loaf.

The Feast of SS. Cosma e Damiano

Stuffing sausage and frying it on Grandma's wood stove

5

Meat, Poultry & Seafood

*M*Y SISTER Beth's recent turn to vegetarianism would have puzzled my grandparents. They grew up in times when the only meat that might be seen all week were a few sausages in the Sunday sauce. In their eyes, having meat on the table was a sign of affluence, insurance against malnutrition. Even during Lent they did not completely abstain from animal products: seafood replaced beef, chicken and pork in sauces, and eggs and cheese were used more often in pasta and sandwiches. Though this was not by any means a terrible hardship, we still rejoiced when meat returned—a glorious roast lamb on Easter Sunday, usually one of Grandpa's own.

My father does a steak on the grill from time to time, but Grandma was much more likely to use meat as part of a dish: ground beef and pork for meatballs or as stuffing for a breast of veal, eggplant, zucchini, peppers or lasagne; chicken stewed in sauce or in soup; round steak rolled into braciole and simmered in sauce; lamb or beef cubes in stew; sausage fried with peppers and onions for a robust sandwich filling; cold cuts sliced thin on an antipasto tray; woodland rabbits and game birds with wine sauce. Not only was her way more inventive and economical, Grandma's meat dishes far surpassed an unadorned roast in flavor. The sauces were enriched by the meat juices and the meats enlivened by the sauces—one instance where the whole was greater than the sum of its parts.

Most of the meat Grandma used came from their own animals, or from animals trapped or hunted in the woods. Fishing, especially for trout, often provided the main course for Friday dinner. Sausage was made at home—even pepperoni for pizza which Grandma cured by looping it over wooden poles suspended in the chill, drafty attic over the kitchen until it reached the correct degree of hardness. No apology was ever made for killing under these circumstances. Though the animals were always well cared for, there was never any confusion in anyone's mind, including us children, about them being kept as pets or for show. To my knowledge, none was ever given a name. They were, quite simply, a means to survival. This did not prevent us from enjoying them and their antics: the spring shearing of the sheep (Grandpa had been a shepherd in Italy) was very interesting to watch—such piles of curly wool, such sleek bodies underneath!

By the time the meat dishes are served at the reunion, the talk has invariably started to drift back over the years. People reminisce about Grandma and Grandpa's fiftieth wedding anniversary (and the lamb done outdoors on skewers to celebrate); fishing trips to Uncle Mike's camp on the Black River up north (and the sensational trout that didn't get away); the dinner parties Mom and Dad used to give professionally when Dad was a sales representative for stainless steel cookware (and their special ways with roast beef and ham); the traditional Christmas Eve fish dinner (seven different kinds, each more delicious than the other)! By and large, the stories are the same every year. And even though we all know the punch lines, the laughter always wells up whenever someone tells a story at someone else's expense. The small children listen to this for a little while, but soon they are restless, starting to tease and pinch one another under the table and feed their scraps to the dogs. So, the mothers let them run off to swim and play while the men set up a poker game. The women clear the table, then settle down to talk over family developments: new babies on the way, who's been sick and with what, job changes, retirements, old neighbors, school and college decisions, and, of course, food. This is my favorite time of the day because the frenzy of getting the meal ready is past. We can finally relax under the trees and appreciate ourselves, slowly sipping glasses of wine while nursing the littlest babies to sleep.

MEAT

Sunday Meatballs

I cannot remember a Sunday in my life when we didn't have pasta (usually spaghetti) and meat sauce (usually with meatballs). At the age of 20 I vowed *never* to make spaghetti and meatballs for my family. I'd had enough of it to last a lifetime. Or so I thought. Now I'm the one at the table, urging my kids to take just a few more bites. If it weren't for these meatballs, I'd never get a drop of tomato sauce into them (they're at that age)! The secret of these meatballs (I've never tasted any as good) is to cook them in the skillet until they are completely encrusted; otherwise, they fall apart in the sauce as they simmer. You want them to absorb the sauce, not thicken it. In our family, Mom would have to make half a recipe extra for us to eat right away; we liked these plain so much we'd have eaten them all that way, leaving none to go into the sauce!

This mixture is also one of the classic stuffings for breast of veal (see p. 114) and for vegetables such as eggplant, zucchini and peppers.

> 4 slices Italian bread, preferably homemade
> Water
> 1 pound lean ground beef (chuck or round)
> 1 pound lean ground pork (ask your butcher to grind
>   this for you if there's none already packaged)
> 3 eggs
> 1 teaspoon parsley flakes
> ½ cup grated Romano cheese
> ½ teaspoon oregano
> 1 clove garlic, minced
> 1½ teaspoons salt
> Olive oil

In a large mixing bowl, soak bread briefly in water. Press out excess water (no water should drip when a slice is handled). Tear bread into very small pieces, no more than ¼-inch across.

Combine bread pieces and all other ingredients except olive oil in large mixing bowl. Stir until the mixture is of uniform texture throughout. Form into balls 1½ inches in diameter.

In a large skillet, pour olive oil to a depth of ½ inch (deep enough so half the meatball cooks at one time and they need be turned only once—this helps prevent them from falling apart while cooking). Place the meatballs in the oil and sauté, uncovered, over medium high heat until the first side is brown and crusty. Remove from heat and let stand five minutes until the meatballs loosen a bit from the bottom of the pan and can be turned without disturbing the crust. Sauté second side until brown and crusty.

Lift from skillet, reserving oil and drippings to brown tomato paste (see Meat Sauce recipe, p. 55), and drain briefly on paper towels. Transfer into sauce you've just started (it needs to be thin to permeate the meatballs) and simmer three more hours. Serve on the side of plates of pasta. Pass grated Romano cheese. Makes approximately two dozen meatballs.

Braciole

A tried-and-true alternative to meatballs—slightly more dressy for company, and, because of the pepper, a bit more spicy:

> 1½ pounds round steak, cut ¼-inch thick (request
>   this cut from your butcher, or flatten a thicker cut
>   with a mallet—this will also tenderize the meat
>   by breaking down many of the tougher fibers)
> Salt
> ½ cup grated Romano cheese
> ¼ cup chopped fresh parsley
> 1 clove garlic, minced
> 1 teaspoon freshly ground black pepper
> Olive oil

Using a large pair of scissors, cut steak into 3- × 5-inch strips. Salt each lightly.

In a small mixing bowl, combine cheese, parsley, garlic and pepper. Sprinkle 1½ tablespoons of cheese mixture over each strip. Roll up each strip into a jellyroll shape, starting at the 3-inch edge. Tie securely with kitchen thread or pierce with three or four toothpicks to hold the rolled shape.

In a large skillet, brown braciole over medium heat in olive oil, as per directions for Meatballs (see p. 105). When braciole are completely browned, add to recipe for meat sauce, reserving oil and drippings for browning tomato paste (see p. 84). When tender, serve with pasta. Pass grated Romano cheese and extra sauce. Makes 18 braciole.

Dinner Party Ham

Interviewers often ask me how I became interested in nutrition, and I have to say it was something I learned from my parents. From 1948 to 1955, when I was three to ten years old, Dad sold "engineered cookware" manufactured by the American Pressed Steel Car Company of Chicago (the same company that manufactured Pullman cars for the railroads). The "waterless cooking" method possible with these triple-clad stainless steel utensils preserves the nutritional value of foods cooked in them. The method involves bringing a small amount of water to a brisk boil, adding vegetables or meat, covering, allowing vapor to build up, then completing the cooking on very low heat. Combining aspects of a minipressure cooker and a steamer, the utensils maintain a boil at less than 212°, so there is less shrinkage of meat and reduced consumption of energy. In addition, nutrients are conserved. We kids took these utensils more or less for granted—getting a charge out of testing the water seal between covers and pans by twirling the knob on top until the covers spun round and round. Mom and Dad gave each of us a full set of the cookware as a wedding present. Only then did we begin to understand its exceptional qualities. I can't imagine cooking in anything else.

To induce people in 1948 to part with $300 for a set of pots and pans took a formidable selling technique. The private dinner party fit the bill. It gave Mom and Dad a chance to demonstrate the equipment in action in the prospective customer's kitchen before a group of the host's friends. This recipe for ham and the next for roast beef were responsible for selling many sets of Permanent!

A 6-pound butt end of ham
2 6-ounce cans tomato paste
2½ cups water
2 tablespoons cornstarch
½ cup water, preferably from cooking vegetables

In a large, heavy stovetop roasting pan, brown ham. In a small mixing bowl, combine water and tomato paste, stirring until smooth. Pour tomato mixture over browned ham. Cover and gradually reduce heat until vapor ceases to escape. Cook two hours or until fork tender. Remove ham from sauce and let rest on a large platter for 15 minutes before slicing very thin.

Combine cornstarch and vegetable cooking water. Add cornstarch mixture gradually to tomato gravy in pan, stirring continuously over low heat until sauce thickens. Arrange ham slices on platter with some of the sauce spooned over them. Serve the remaining sauce over an accompanying dish of cooked cabbage, rice or potatoes. Serves 8.

Dinner Party Roast Beef

A 6-pound top or bottom round roast, trimmed very
    lean
Garlic salt
3 medium onions, diced
½ pound Italian sausage, sweet or hot
½ pound lean ground beef (chuck or round)
1 cup canned button mushrooms and canning water
1 teaspoon garlic salt
3 cups water, preferably from cooking vegetables
¼ cup cornstarch

Sprinkle garlic salt liberally over surface of roast. Transfer roast and a few strips of suet trimmings to large, heavy stovetop roasting pan. Over moderate heat, brown roast over entire surface, then remove from pan and let rest on platter.

Remove casings from sausage meat. In a large skillet, combine meat with onions, ground beef and garlic salt. Sauté over moderate heat until the meat is thoroughly browned and onions are transparent. Place sausage mixture into roasting pan, stirring until juices from the roast and the thin crust from the bottom of the pan are incorporated into the mixture. Add mushrooms and their canning water. Stir thoroughly, then bring to the boiling point. Return roast to the pan, resting it on top of the sausage mixture. Cover and reduce heat until vapor ceases to escape (very low). Simmer for two hours or until roast is fork tender. Remove meat from pan and let rest 15 minutes before slicing very thin.

Add 2½ cups vegetable cooking water to remaining sausage mixture in the pan. Stir thoroughly. Dissolve cornstarch in remaining ½ cup vegetable cooking water. Bring gravy to boiling point, then add cornstarch mixture, stirring continuously until gravy thickens and becomes golden. Bits of the ground beef and sausage add texture to the finished gravy— do not strain them out.

Serve the roast arranged on a platter with gravy spooned over the slices. Save some of the gravy to go over accompanying small potatoes cooked in their skins. Serves 8.

Elsie's Beef Soup

If it weren't for the broth, this would qualify as a pot roast, there's so much meat in it. Whenever Mom knows we're coming for a visit, she'll make a pot of this to be steaming hot when we arrive. There's nothing like walking in out of the blustery cold on a Christmas week night and sitting down at the table to a big bowl of this. Even my seven-year-old daughter Ginevra, who's not big on soups, asks for seconds!

    5 quarts water
    A 3-pound chuck roast, with bones in
    1½ cups canned tomatoes
    6 whole carrots, peeled
    2 medium onions, chopped
    2 stalks celery, with leaves
    2 teaspoons parsley flakes
    1 tablespoon salt
    ⅛ teaspoon black pepper, freshly ground
    1 pound cooked rice, small macaroni (ditalini, acini di
        pepe), or greens
    Romano cheese, grated

Place all ingredients in large kettle. Bring to boiling point and skim foam from surface. Cover, reduce heat, and simmer over low heat for another two hours. Remove cover and simmer one more hour.

Place cooked rice, macaroni, or greens in a large serving bowl or tureen. Remove meat and vegetables and arrange on a serving platter. Pour broth over rice, macaroni, or greens in tureen and serve at once. Pass grated Romano cheese, thick slices of Italian bread, and fresh butter. Serves 8.

Esther Virgilio's Roast Leg of Lamb

My father's cousin Esther is the family expert on lamb. Even people outside the family often ask her for this recipe, our Easter favorite, and the main course at Grandma and Grandpa's 50th wedding anniversary.

A 5 to 6-pound leg of lamb
¼ cup chopped fresh parsley
½ cup grated Romano cheese
Salt
Black pepper, freshly ground *or* red pepper flakes
Rind of one lemon, grated
4 cloves garlic, peeled and slivered
¼ cup olive oil
3 bay leaves

Trim most of the brittle fat (the fell) from the lamb. In a small bowl, combine parsley, cheese, salt, pepper and lemon rind to make a filling mixture. Make a dozen evenly spaced slits in the skin of the roast. Into each slit, press a sliver of garlic and a bit of the filling. Rub all over with olive oil and place in a roasting pan, fat side up. Lay bay leaves on top. Roast at 350° for three hours in the middle of the oven, basting with pan drippings every half hour. Serve with Italian arborio rice or brown rice, dressed with butter, and a side dish of Mixed Summer Vegetables (see p. 81).

Lamb on a Skewer

A wonderful way to do lamb outdoors—one of the sure signs of spring!

¾ cup olive oil
¾ cup dry red wine
1 teaspoon salt
½ teaspoon black pepper, freshly ground
2 pounds lamb, cut in 2-inch cubes
Garlic salt

Combine the olive oil, wine, salt and pepper in a shallow roasting pan. Marinate the lamb cubes in this mixture for three hours, turning every half hour so all sides of the meat are tenderized. Fix cubes on 6 skewers and sprinkle each liberally with garlic salt. Roast over live coals or under broiler until browned, turning often to cook evenly and thoroughly. Check a center piece after 20 minutes to see if meat is done. Serve on a bed of rice and pass mint jelly. Serves 6.

Feast Day Liver

Skewers of this go like hotcakes from the street stalls during the Feast of SS. Cosma and Damiano. Now you can make them yourself!

¾ pound pork caul *(rete)*
3 cups warm water
½ cup vinegar
2 pounds fresh pork liver, cut into 2-inch pieces
¼ teaspoon fennel seeds
Salt
Black pepper, freshly ground
Juice of two lemons
20 bay leaves (approximately)
Olive oil

Obtain caul fat from an Italian butcher or specialty store. The caul is easily torn, so soak it in warm water and vinegar to make it more pliable before you start to work with it. Cut caul with sharp scissors into 20 4-inch pieces.

Arrange liver pieces in a single layer on a platter. Sprinkle them with fennel, salt, pepper and lemon juice. Inside each piece of caul, wrap a piece of liver and a bay leaf. Fix wrapped cubes onto six skewers and grill over live coals, charcoal, or under a broiler for 6 to 8 minutes. Baste with olive oil once or twice to prevent liver from drying out. Liver should be just cooked through. Serve at once. Excellent with Stuffed Hot Cherry Peppers or Stuffed Tomatoes (see p. 35 and p. 80).

Stuffed Veal Roast

An elegant company dinner dish that's nowhere near as much work as it looks!

4-pound breast or shoulder of veal, boneless
1 clove garlic, peeled
½ recipe of Sunday Meatballs (see p. 105)
Olive oil
1 cup (approximately) water, chicken stock or white
    wine

Ask your butcher to cut a pocket into the breast or shoulder to accommodate your stuffing. Rub the outside of the roast with garlic, then drop clove into the batch of stuffing to be placed inside the veal. Fill the pocket with the meatball mixture. Sew pocket opening with needle and coarse thread or use skewers to hold shut. Rub olive oil over surface of the roast.

Preheat oven to 450°. Place veal in an oiled roasting pan in the middle of the oven until meat starts to brown. Reduce heat to 375° and add basting liquid (veal has very little of its own fat). Baste every 20 minutes, or, if you prefer, brush on more olive oil halfway through the cooking procedure. Roast one more hour, then transfer to a platter. Let rest 10 minutes before slicing into portions ½-inch thick. Potatoes, pan-fried (see p. 96), scalloped, or as gnocchi (see p. 97) make a delicious accompaniment. Serves 8.

Veal Scaloppine

Though the price of veal cutlets certainly removes this dish from the economy class, eating pasta a few days a week makes an indulgence like this possible once in a while.

4 veal cutlets, soaked in milk overnight in the
    refrigerator
1 egg yolk
1 tablespoon water
1 cup crumbs (from day-old Italian bread or crackers)
¼ cup minced parsley
¼ teaspoon garlic powder
4 teaspoons butter, melted
4 lemon slices

Pound cutlets with a mallet to the degree of thinness you prefer, being careful not to shred the fibers of the meat. In a medium-sized mixing bowl combine all remaining ingredients except lemon slices. Stir until mixture is of even texture throughout. Dip each cutlet into the mixture, coating both sides, then place in oiled baking pan. Place lemon slice on top of each cutlet. Bake in 350° oven for one hour, or until nicely browned. Serve with Roasted Peppers (see p. 32), Mushroom Stew (see p. 94), or Greens and Beans (see p. 90). Serves 4.

Veal Parmesan

A variation of Veal Scaloppine, above, made by substituting ½ cup grated Parmesan cheese for ½ cup of the bread or cracker crumbs. Otherwise, proceed in the same way. Serve this with Tomato Sauce (see p. 53).

SAUSAGE

IT WOULD be hard to imagine a reunion without sausage: fried sausage and pepper sandwiches to eat while everything else is being readied; tomato sauce given an extra zing by being simmered with browned sausage; slices of pepperoni festooning a pizza; sausage coils that have been stored in oil and grilled over the pit; small chunks of sausage meat, browned and stirred through a bowl of macaroni; juicy links bursting their casings settled proudly off to the side of a platter piled high with steaming spaghetti. As the song says, "Who could ask for anything more?"

After years of buying sausage at Italian specialty stores, my mother and Aunt Esther have rediscovered the rewards of making sausage at home. At the reunion, people ask, "Now, which is yours, Elsie?" or "Where's Esther's?," holding off until they can get some of the homemade.

There are two decisions to be made about a batch of sausage: will it be sweet or hot, and will it be used right away (fresh) or cured for later (hard). A great deal of sausage can be made very quickly by four people with a bit of experience (one to chop, one to mix, one to feed the machine and one to hold the casings while they fill). But speed isn't really the point. With the ever-increasing number of additives, fillers, preservatives and questionable chemicals on the labels of the commercial brands, the triumph of making sausage at home is that you control what goes into it. Not only can you select better grades of meat, thereby insuring a better flavor, you can feel at peace with yourself when you serve it to your family. Pork products have developed a bad reputation because of the ways they are routinely processed in this country, but they are really excellent foods, very high in the B vitamins and, when trimmed of extra fat, high in protein, too. These days Mom doesn't air dry sausage as Grandma did. She freezes it instead. If all pork products were handled the same way, the need to preserve them chemically would be eliminated.

A sausage-making session takes place in my mother's kitchen two or three times a year. There's fun in the process, but the best part is the eating!

Sweet Sausage Patties

4 pounds pork shoulder, boneless
2 teaspoons fennel seeds
2 teaspoons salt
2½ tablespoons freshly ground black pepper

Trim most of the fat from the pork shoulder. Cut the pork into cubes about ¼-inch across and combine in a large mixing bowl with seasonings. Force a small amount of pork mixture through a grinder/filler machine with a coarse blade attachment. To taste-test, shape a small amount of mixture into a patty and fry in a skillet until browned. Cool, then taste. Correct seasoning in the rest of the batch before proceeding. Force the rest of the mixture, a small amount at a time, through the machine and form into patties. To store, place each in its own plastic bag and freeze. Easy to use as an accompaniment to breakfast eggs or to brown and crumble as an addition to pasta dishes. Makes 20 patties.

Sweet Sausage in Coils or Links

One recipe Sweet Sausage (above)
String
3 or 4 sections hog casings (usually found in the
    refrigerator section of the market, near hot dogs;
    otherwise, ask your butcher to order you some)

To prepare casings, remove sections from their salt-packed container. They will appear dried out and brittle. Run cool faucet water over and through each casing to rinse off salt. Soak casings in a pan of cold water for another hour before using. Drain and pat dry.

Tie casing with string at one end and attach the open end to a sausage-stuffing machine or the end of a funnel with a large-diameter spout. Force the sausage mixture through the machine or funnel, maintaining steady pressure so the mixture fills the casing smoothly with no air pockets. A second person can help by smoothing the casing around the filling as you work and supporting the weight of the sausage so the casing doesn't tear. If you like, tie the length of sausage every 3 or 4 inches to make links. We usually leave the coils in one long length. Repeat with as many casings as necessary to process your batch of sausage mixture. If an air bubble should develop, a fine needle inserted into the casing will usually release the air without causing a tear.

Fresh sausage may be kept in the refrigerator, closely wrapped in plastic, for use within two days. Or, wrap in airtight bags and freeze. Thaw sausage in the refrigerator for 12 hours before using. Makes 4 pounds.

Hot Sausage

To recipe for Sweet Sausage (see p. 118), add:

1 teaspoon hot red pepper flakes (more if your taste prefers)

Process as patties, coils or links and use in any recipe calling for sausage. Many people love this in sauce.

Beef and Pork Sausage

Modify Sweet Sausage recipe (see p. 118) by substituting for half the pork shoulder:

2½ pounds beef round, chopped into ¼-inch cubes

Makes a chewier sausage that adds extra richness to sauce—like having both meatballs and sausage.

Grandma's Pepperoni

Late in fall, suspend a wooden pole at least 3 inches in diameter in a chilly (but not freezing), *well-ventilated* room (an unheated sunporch might work well). Loop lengths of Hot Sausage (see above) over the pole so that they do not touch one another and so that there are no sharp bends in any of them. Let sausage hang there until it reaches the desired degree of hardness. Left for three months, it becomes pepperoni. Slice into thin rounds and use as a pizza topping, an all-time favorite.

Angie Argento Crescenza's Hot Sausage in Oil

My mother gives this her highest praise, "the best ever!"

2 pounds hot Italian sausage, 60 percent dried, but
     not as hard as pepperoni
Olive oil

Cut sausage in lengths to fit the height of a two-quart glass canning jar. Fit sausage snugly into jar and fill to the brim with oil. Make sure the sausage is completely covered. Store at least one month.

When you are ready to cook sausage, place it and the oil in which it was stored into a large skillet. Brown to the point of crispness over medium heat (there should be no pink meat left in the center). Remove sausages, reserving oil and drippings to fry onions and peppers for garnish or side dishes. Drain sausages briefly on paper towels. Serve on hard rolls or slices of homemade Italian bread. Serves 6.

CHICKEN

*L*OOKING AFTER the White Leghorns, all 60 of them, was Grandma's job, with assistance from the children. Grandpa grew hard corn for the chickens and took it to the miller to have it cracked, but it was Grandma and the kids who spread it every day along with some laying mash to encourage optimal egg production. The kids also picked the eggs and loaded them into crates to be delivered to Utica markets.

When I was very small, I liked to toss corn through the fence of the chicken run, but nothing could bring me to walk inside the fence to scatter the feed. *Those chickens pecked!* How I admired Grandma's courage as she strode fearlessly into the pen, holding the corn in her skirts with one hand, reaching in and flinging it down with the other. It impressed me that, for some reason, no chicken ever *dared* peck at her. Perhaps they knew that if they gave her any trouble, they'd become candidates for her famous soup!

Needless to say, the only chickens that ever appeared on Grandma's table were ones she raised and killed herself. Her method for removing the feathers: immerse the freshly killed and drained bird in a pan of boiling water until the feathers loosen. Remove from the water and pluck at once. Clean the cavity, rinse inside and out, then use in the recipe of your choice.

For reliable information on selecting a good chicken (or any other kind of meat, for that matter) at the market, check Nikki and David Goldbeck's *The Supermarket Handbook: Access to Whole Foods* (New York: Harper and Row, 1973).

Chicken and
Potatoes in the Oven

Grandma's answer to Sunday dinner for a gang.

7 medium potatoes, peeled and quartered
5 medium onions, peeled and quartered
6 large carrots, peeled and quartered
2 tablespoons fresh parsley, chopped
4 chicken breasts
6 chicken legs
Salt and black pepper, freshly ground

Fill large kettle with water to a depth of 2 inches and bring to boil. Arrange vegetables in layers in the kettle—onions first, potatoes in the middle, and carrots on top. Cover and steam until potatoes are partially cooked (about 20 minutes).

Oil a large, shallow baking pan and fill with vegetables. Salt and pepper liberally and garnish with parsley. Arrange chicken pieces on top of vegetables so they form a complete cover. Salt and pepper liberally. Bake one hour at 350° in the middle of the oven. Juices from the chicken will baste the underlying vegetables, so there is no need to add water. Turn the chicken pieces after half an hour, or when they are well browned. Serve in the baking dish, or place chicken on a platter and vegetables in another bowl. Serves 6.

Fried Chicken, My Way

An Italian-accented alternative to carry-out chicken. The coating mixture works equally well on cod or flounder.

     12 pieces chicken (breasts, legs, thighs)
     2 eggs, beaten slightly
     1 tablespoon milk
     1 tablespoon water
     2 tablespoons minced fresh parsley
     ¾ cup whole wheat flour
     ¼ cup corn meal
     2 teaspoons garlic powder
     2 teaspoons onion powder
     1 teaspoon salt
     ½ teaspoon freshly ground black pepper
     ½ teaspoon paprika
     Corn oil

Rinse chicken parts, then pat dry with paper towels. In a medium-sized mixing bowl, combine eggs, milk and water. In another medium-sized bowl, stir together all remaining ingredients except the oil.

Fill a large, heavy skillet with corn oil to a depth of 2 inches. Bring to a high temperature adequate for frying—to test, drop in a bit of flour. If it makes the oil bubble up, sizzling, it's ready. Do not heat to the point of smoking.

Dip each piece of chicken successively in the egg mixture, then roll in the flour mixture, then place into the skillet. Fry until well browned and crispy (approximately 8 minutes on each side). Drain on paper towels. Serve with corn-on-the-cob, green beans in sauce, or young peas. Serves 6.

Chicken in Sauce

A quick supper if you have some leftover sauce. Follow the recipe for Meat Sauce (see p. 55), adding two 3-pound frying chickens, cut up and sautéed in olive oil until golden brown, to the sauce for the last hour of simmering. Serve the chicken pieces on a large platter and combine the sauce thoroughly with pasta. Pass grated Romano cheese. Serves 6.

Chicken Soup

Grandma had all her babies at home with Doctor Rossi from Utica and her sister-in-law, Anna Sforza Virgilio, a midwife trained in Italy, attending her. Just last year, a group of researchers announced their finding that chicken soup promotes healing. Grandma would have told them not to waste good money studying the obvious: chicken soup has been the traditional first food after childbirth for generations of Italian women for just that very reason! Without her own mother there to cook for her and keep her house for awhile, Grandma depended on Anna's experience (she had nine children of her own) and help in those early days with her new infants. I presume that one of Anna's prime responsibilities was to make this soup.

When I was born, Grandma had some of this ready for my mother. And when I gave birth to my first two girls, Marisa and Ginevra, Mom was there each time with a steaming potful the day I came home from the hospital.

My last two babies, Cornelia and Thomas, were born at home with their father, an obstetrician, helping me.

I called my mother and father an hour after each home birth to tell them the good news. I can remember the end of both of those conversations: someone coming into the room and asking me what I wanted to eat. My reply, "Chicken soup!" Grandma would have been proud.

5 quarts water
A 3½ pound broiling chicken, cut up
6 whole carrots, peeled
2 medium onions, chopped
2 stalks celery with leaves
2 teaspoons parsley flakes
1 tablespoon salt
⅛ teaspoon black pepper, freshly ground
1 bay leaf
2 cups cooked rice or small pasta (pastina, ditalini, acini de pepe)
½ cup grated Romano cheese

Pour water into a large, heavy kettle and add chicken, carrots, onions, celery, parsley flakes, salt, pepper and bay leaf. Cover and bring to a boil over high heat. Reduce heat and simmer, covered, for three hours or until meat seems about to fall from the bone.

Remove chicken and vegetables from broth and serve on a separate platter. Place cooked rice or pasta in a large serving bowl or tureen. Strain the broth and pour over rice or pasta in tureen. Serve at once with grated cheese. Makes 4 quarts.

Stracciatella

A quick lunchtime soup or first course for dinner.

1 quart strained chicken broth, preferably homemade (see above)
3 egg whites
¼ cup grated Romano cheese
4 teaspoons chopped fresh parsley

In a medium-sized saucepan, bring broth to a full boil. Pour in egg whites in a steady stream, holding their container with one hand and stirring them vigorously into the broth with a whisk or fork in the other hand. Remove from heat as soon as they form white strands. Overcooking makes them rubbery. Serve at once in bowls, garnished with cheese and parsley. Serves 4.

Sautéed Rabbit or Game Birds with Wine

One of Grandma's winter specialties, featuring Grandpa's own wine.

1 quart water
4 tablespoons vinegar
1 rabbit, cleaned *or*
1 pound game bird meat, boneless
½ cup olive oil
1½ to 2 cups dry red wine
Salt and black pepper, freshly ground

Combine water and vinegar in a mixing bowl and rinse rabbit or birds inside and out in it. Dry carefully and cut into serving pieces as you would a chicken.

In a large skillet, heat the olive oil to the point of fragrance. Place meat pieces in skillet and add ½ cup of wine. Salt and pepper to taste. Reduce heat and sauté, uncovered, adding small amounts of wine whenever necessary to prevent meat from drying out. Turn pieces of meat often to cook evenly. Check for tenderness with a fork after 20 minutes. Depending on the size and age of the rabbit, you may need to cook an additional 10 to 15 minutes.

Remove meat from pan and drain on paper towels. Serve on a platter with boiled potatoes in their skins or with whole wheat noodles. Serves 4.

SEAFOOD

Black River Trout

For years Uncle Mike had a camp up north, near Boonville, on the Black River. Like the ads used to say, getting there was half the fun. We'd drive up from Utica on a Saturday morning, stopping in at the quaint old soda fountain in town for a sundae or milk shake, then turning left just after a stand of bushes marking what appeared to be someone's driveway but turned out to be a sandy, bumpy, deeply-rutted road that paralleled the river's edge. The farther in we drove, the closer in the bushes grew—scraping along the windshield and sides of the car and snapping through the open windows, until the road completely gave out in a sandy clearing under scores of towering pines.

The camp was off to the right and beyond it, the river— swift running current, massive black boulders, crashing white spray—a constant, tumultuous roar that forced us to speak in booming voices in order to be understood. The men would get on their hip boots and go charging out into the middle of the torrent, lugging along their tackle. My mother, who loved to swim, would take us kids down to a small lagoon that pooled below the camp's screened porch, and there we'd spend an idyllic afternoon—a whole river all to ourselves.

An hour or so before dinner, we'd hike to a spring to fill our water jugs and collect kindling from the pine woods for our outdoor fireplace. There was a kerosene stove inside (used mainly to make breakfast coffee), but a large part of the appeal of the place was its rusticity: no running water, no indoor toilet facilities, no telephone, no mail delivery, no television, no neighbors, just pine trees everywhere. Over the coals of the wood fire, we'd cook fish the men had caught, steam corn brought from town, and flame marshmallows on long green sticks for dessert.

To this day, the smell of pines transports me back to those camping days—and to those fish suppers!

> 4 to 6 brook (brown) trout, each 6 to 8 inches long
> ½ cup salted butter
> Black pepper, freshly ground

Remove heads and fins from trout, but leave tails on. Clean insides, then rinse inside and out with cold water. Pat dry.

Melt butter in a large, heavy skillet (Uncle Mike preferred cast iron) over a charcoal fire. Add trout and sauté on first side until quite brown. Turn and do the other side until the whole is quite firm and well-browned. Serve to 4 after grinding some fresh pepper on top.

Alternatively, dab butter on top of each fish. Wrap each in a separate piece of aluminum foil. Place on barbecue grill over charcoal fire and cook for 5 or 6 minutes on each side. Pepper to taste.

Christmas Eve
Fish Fry

The oysters and clams that kick off the reunion celebration, the shrimp cocktail my mother likes so much, the fried codfish *(baccalà)* and smelts that come later in the day, the squid *(calamari)* that Uncle Fred gets Aunt Esther to make with some linguine, and the sardines some people like as side dishes are also seen together on one other menu during the year: the traditional Christmas Eve fish fry. Depending on family preference, a wide variety of seafood might be served, but the number of courses was usually kept to seven (some people say in reference to the seven sacraments). At our cousins', the Argentos', eel, squid, octopus, whiting, cod, mackerel and sardines were prepared. Most other Italian families also did eel, but Grandma hated it, so we never had any. Instead, our family looked forward to the shrimp, a delicacy either boiled or deep fried—and affordable, too, at 20¢ a pound! My father remembers going to Durante's grocery, corner of Jay and Pelleteri Avenue, East Utica, a day or two before Christmas, helping to bring home the load of fish, clams and oysters. Aunt Toni remembers Grandma standing for hours at her huge black stove, frying and frying away until nobody could eat another bite. All of this is somewhat amusing to recount since this was supposed to be a day of fasting (no meat) before feasting on Christmas. However, I've yet to taste a goose, duck, ham or turkey that could compare to a lineup of clams, oysters, shrimp, *baccalà*, squid, sardines and smelts!

Clams and Oysters

Recipes for these are in Chapter 2, Antipasti (see pp. 24-27).

Boiled Shrimp

4 quarts water or beer
1½ teaspoons salt
5 pounds medium to large fresh or frozen shrimp, in
        the shell
Cracked ice

Bring water to boil over high heat in a large kettle. Add salt and shrimp. If fresh, reduce heat to a simmer and cook 4 minutes. If frozen, keep on high heat until water returns to a boil, then reduce heat and cook 4 minutes. Shrimp should not be overcooked. They should be pink, but not curled up. Drain at once, then run cold water over shrimp continuously until they are cool enough to handle. Drain. Remove shells by holding the tail and tugging firmly on the rest of the shell body. Discard shells. Remove dark vein that runs the length of the back by slicing partway through the shrimp with a very sharp knife and using the knife point to dislodge the vein. Rinse and refrigerate until thoroughly chilled. Place a mound of cracked ice into a large serving bowl and arrange shrimp on top of it. Serve with lemon wedges and Cocktail Sauce to 8.

Cocktail Sauce

¾ cup ketchup
¼ cup grated horseradish

Combine in small bowl. Makes one cup.

Fried Shrimp

5 pounds medium to large shrimp, in the shell
2 cups pancake mix (Grandma liked Aunt Jemima
    brand)
¼ cup minced fresh parsley
1 teaspoon salt
1 teaspoon garlic powder
Corn oil

Remove shells from shrimp and devein as described in method for Boiled Shrimp (above). Combine pancake mix, parsley, salt and garlic powder in a large mixing bowl. Roll each of the shrimp in the coating mixture.

Bring corn oil to high temperature, but not smoking, in a large heavy skillet. Oil should be at least 2 inches deep. Arrange some of the coated shrimp in the skillet and fry until golden brown. To keep finished shrimp hot while the rest of the batch is cooking, place in 250° oven on shallow baking sheet. Repeat frying process until all shrimp are done. Serve with lemon wedges and Cocktail Sauce (see above). Serves 8.

Fried Codfish
(Baccalà)

2 pounds fresh *or* 1 pound dried and salted codfish
    fillets
1 cup saltine cracker crumbs, rolled very fine
1 cup unbleached flour
2 tablespoons grated Romano cheese
¼ teaspoon freshly ground black pepper
¼ teaspoon oregano
⅛ teaspoon garlic salt
1 egg, beaten
½ cup milk
Corn oil

If using dried, salted cod, soak for 48 hours, changing water every 8 hours, in a glass, enamel or stainless steel pan. Then prepare just as for the 2 pounds fresh fish.

Cut cod into serving portions for 8 people.

In a large mixing bowl, combine crumbs, flour, cheese, pepper, oregano and garlic salt. In another bowl, mix egg and milk. Dip each piece of fish first into egg mixture, then coat with crumb mixture. Set aside on large platter.

In a large, heavy skillet, pour corn oil to a depth of ½ inch and set over medium high heat. Gently transfer pieces of fish into oil and allow to brown completely on one side before turning (this reduces the chances of the fish falling to bits from repeated turnings). Turn with large spatula and repeat with second side. Total cooking time should be about 20 minutes. Drain fish on paper towels. Serve hot with lemon wedges. Serves 8.

Squid (Calamari)

 2 pounds squid, cleaned and pounded to tenderize
 2 medium onions, sliced thin
 ½ cup olive oil
 3 cups ripe Italian plum tomatoes, fresh or canned
 1 bay leaf
 1 small chili pepper, minced

Cut squid tentacles into rounds approximately 1½ inches wide and the body into similar-sized squares. In a large skillet, sauté the onions in the olive oil until they are soft and transparent. Add tomatoes, bay leaf and chili pepper, stirring until well combined and tomatoes begin to soften. Simmer 10 minutes over low heat. Add squid and simmer 15 additional minutes or until squid are tender. Serve over linguine or spaghetti to 4.

Fried Smelts

 1 pound smelts, cleaned
 2 to 3 cups olive oil
 1 cup pancake mix

Rinse smelts and pat dry. Dip in olive oil, then roll in pancake mix. Place remaining oil in deep fryer or deep saucepan and bring to high temperature (370°). Add smelts and fry for three minutes or until golden brown. Serve at once with lemon wedges to 4.

Picking strawberries with the cousins

6

Fruits & Nuts

ON ANY day but Sunday our family meals end with fruit. But since the reunion is always held on Sunday, the fruit course is what the kids get when they come straggling back to the table around four o'clock after running three-legged races, tossing water balloons, and making countless leaps into the swimming pool. It's also what a grownup might content himself with while awaiting the really sweet desserts *(dolci)* and coffee.

Served simply, the ripe fruit of the season might just be eaten out of hand, selected from a chilled bowlful resting in the middle of the table. Or, it might be sliced and combined with fresh juices in a fruit cup, baked, or set off with some sweetened cream. If we're lucky, someone will bring figs and soft dates stuffed with walnuts or almonds.

Fruit can add eye-appeal to light breads, and there's sure to be a variety of fruits put up in jars of light syrup (used during the winter for pie filling, but more likely to top a dish of ice cream in the summer).

Honeydew Melon with Prosciutto

Honeydews were Grandma's favorite. A really ripe honeydew has firm flesh that melts into refreshing sweetness when you take a bite. The salty accent of the prosciutto makes an inspired combination. If you open a melon and the flesh is soft or looks waterlogged, it's past its peak—don't waste your prosciutto on it.

1 ripe honeydew melon
12 slices prosciutto

Cut melon in half. Scoop out and discard seeds. Cut each half into six slices, then cut away rind. Wrap each melon section with a strip of prosciutto, fastening it with a toothpick. Serve chilled to 12.

STRAWBERRIES

*T*O MOST people June is the month for brides, but to us it means strawberries. Our family has been carrying on a love affair with strawberries ever since Grandpa planted his first two-acre patch back in 1930. These days no reunion would be complete without berries: strawberries and cream, strawberry shortcake, strawberry pie, Italian sponge cake with strawberry topping, and strawberry jam for Pizza Fritte. But, to tell the truth, nothing surpasses the way the kids like them best—right out in the field, just plucked from the plant with little berry-stained fingers, and popped whole into their mouths.

Picking strawberries is a skill learned very early in our family. I couldn't have been more than eight the first time I was allowed to spend a week of my summer vacation at Grandma's helping with the berries. How slowly the last weeks of school passed that year! How eager I was to get my chance in the strawberry patch! Small children and serious berry picking did not mix, at least not in Grandpa's eyes. Oh, the little kids might be tolerated at the end of a row that had been pretty much picked out by the end of the season—and it was thrilling to fill even half a basket with the smaller berries our mothers used for jam. But working all the way down your own row, picking for market, that was something else. That was for real—for money—a clear sign of increasing ability to handle responsibility, a step toward maturity.

If I had even a tiny flicker of an idea that berry picking was just a lark, a way to get a nice suntan, it was quickly dispelled on the first day. Grandpa spent a few minutes schooling me in how to move aside the shady, green leaves of the plants and lift the clusters of berries for close inspection. I learned not to pick berries with white tips, pale backsides, or (the worst) dark, mushy spots. Any overly ripe berries were to be removed from the plants to stop them from taking any more nutrients that might better find their way into the berries still developing.

He taught me the proper way to fill a basket (rounded on top to give a generous measure for the customer's money, but not so full as to squash the top berries when the baskets were loaded into crates). Each basket was to look just so. Grandpa was as fussy about the strawberries as he was about the tomatoes, or any other crop that left the farm with our name associated with it. All new pickers, young or old, relatives or not, had to work under the watchful eye of an old hand until their work was up to Grandpa's standards. He checked every basket every day before issuing little colored tickets representing how many quarts you'd turned in. He was understanding the first time around—willing to dump out two boxes, throw out the unfit pieces, then replace the good ones in one basket—but anyone who didn't catch on by the second carrier of eight baskets (still picking green ones, underfilling, overfilling) would be bounced from the patch with an irate lecture. Grandpa took such affronts personally and felt he had plenty to do without being put upon by a *chooch* (jackass)! You always knew exactly where you stood with Grandpa. He didn't mince words and diplomacy was not his strong suit. Turning out gorgeous produce was. This uncompromising attitude brought customers to the farm in droves every June— and still does, since my father behaves in just about the same way.

Though many Italian women and their children picked for Grandpa, the all-time strawberry picker par excellence was Jenny Maxwell from the farmhouse up at the corner of the Beacon Light Road. She could out-pick everyone, man or woman, for miles around. A hundred quarts a day was her regular pace—and she didn't just skim a row, taking all the big ones to fill her baskets quickly. Once Jenny had been down a row, nobody else would find anything pickable in it until the next day or the one after that! To pick strawberries like Jenny was one of those goals parents always seemed to encourage their children to strive for. Though we all agreed it was absolutely unattainable, we gave it our best. For myself, I was ecstatic to leave the field each day with 50 cents (25 quarts worth), a small fortune to me in 1953.

Today things are a bit different. Dad has six times as many acres in strawberries and three different varieties (Early Dawn, Sparkle and Catskill). But the biggest change is the "pick your own" style of operation. A small announcement at the beginning of the season, and it's wall-to-wall people around the farm for the next month. They begin to queue up for carriers and baskets about 7 in the morning, even though my father doesn't step outside until 8. From the front porch he delivers a five-minute oration-exhortation to the multitude about how to pick the berries without trampling the plants; then, Pied Piper-style, he leads the throng to the field for the day and assigns rows, just as Grandpa used to do. But what happens when Dad leaves the field to go back to the house and meet the next group would make Grandpa blanch. People soon break ranks and start dashing madly about in search of the biggest, absolutely perfect strawberries—which always appear to be in *that* row over there, just two away from this one—leaving the rest of the berries to the few pickers Dad employs to provide berries-by-the-quart for the roadside stand.

By 11 or 12, it's a full-fledged circus out front with people waiting to get weighed in (Dad sells by the pound), the midday pickers just arriving, the telephone ringing as people special order so many quarts for their church social or wedding reception, and Dad having a fit every time he notices somebody way out in the field skip another row! By 3 in the afternoon the rows are exhausted and so are we. Dad hangs the sign "Picked out" on one of the maple trees and retires to the porch to deal with the trickle of people who show up right until sundown asking for a chance to get a quart or two for their ailing grandmothers or that night's dessert. Despite the frenzy, it's a great time of year. Everybody in the family pitches in at one time or another, and we get to see people we haven't run into since last year at strawberry time.

Overnight, more berries ripen, we refresh ourselves with sound sleep in the country air, and in the morning we're ready to do it all over again. And what do we do before going to bed? Eat strawberries, of course!

Strawberries and Cream

1 quart strawberries
2 cups heavy cream
Sugar or honey

Place strawberries in a large colander or strainer and run cold water over them, turning gently to remove all sand. Turn out on paper towels to drain. Remove green stem end with the point of a paring knife or by pinching the leaves between thumb and forefinger of one hand and twisting the fruit with the other. Slice in halves, and place in large serving bowl. Pour cream over, then add sugar or honey to taste. Serve in small cups to 4.

Strawberry Shortcake

2 cups unbleached flour
3 teaspoons baking powder
1½ teaspoons salt
1½ tablespoons sugar
¼ cup butter
⅞ cup milk
3 cups strawberries, cleaned
½ cup clover honey or sugar
1 cup heavy cream
1 tablespoon vanilla extract

In a large mixing bowl, sift flour, baking powder, salt and sugar. Cut in butter with a fork until the mixture is of even texture throughout (beads about the size of small peas). Add milk and stir just until moistened. Turn out onto floured work surface. Knead gently for one minute, then roll to a thickness of one inch. Cut with a 2- or 2½-inch biscuit cutter or open end of a water glass. Bake at 450° on ungreased cookie sheet for 12 minutes. Makes 12 biscuits.

Alternatively, roll out to thickness of one inch and bake as one large shortcake, approximately 20 minutes.

In a mixing bowl, partially crush strawberries to release some juice. Add sugar or honey and correct sweetness (it will depend on the natural sweetness in your berries).

In another bowl, whip heavy cream until it forms soft peaks. Add vanilla, then beat until cream stands in stiff peaks.

To assemble shortcake, place two biscuits in bottom of individual bowl, spoon on strawberries and juice and top with whipped cream. Or, place large biscuit on shallow serving dish, add berries and top with peaks of whipped cream. Divide into portions at the table. Serves 6.

Strawberry Pie

Crust:

1⅔ cups graham cracker crumbs
¼ cup butter, at room temperature
1 egg, beaten

In a small mixing bowl, combine all ingredients and blend with a fork or fingertips until mixture is uniform. Turn out into an ungreased 9-inch pie tin and with fingertips press into an even-layered crust covering bottom and sides. Or, press an 8-inch pie tin into the 9-inch tin to achieve an even-layered crust. Bake at 375° for 8 minutes. Cool to room temperature.

Filling:

2 cups strawberries, cleaned
1 cup strawberry preserves, preferably homemade

Combine ingredients in a bowl and spoon into baked pie crust. Refrigerate for 30 minutes.

Topping:

1 cup heavy cream
½ cup unsweetened coconut, toasted

In a small mixing bowl, whip cream until stiff. Spoon over pie filling. Sprinkle coconut shreds over top. Serve cold to 8.

Strawberry Jam

Spread on a piece of toast or a cornmeal muffin in the dead of winter, this jam never fails to take me back to June at home, making jam with my mother on a perfect afternoon. This quick-boil method preserves the fresh fruit taste.

2 quarts ripe strawberries, cleaned and crushed
7 cups sugar
½ bottle fruit pectin (Mom prefers Certo)

In a large, heavy saucepan mix sugar and strawberries, then bring to a boil. Boil for one minute, then stir in pectin. Spoon into sterilized pint jars and cool to room temperature. Seal with a thin layer of melted paraffin or follow directions for your metal lids. Makes approximately 10 pints.

Frozen Strawberries

Hard as we try, there are always more berries than we can eat in one month. Now that Mom has a big home freezer the problem has become academic. We can enjoy frozen berries the year round. Mom's serving hint: spoon over ice cream, shortcake or sponge cake when berries are *just thawed,* otherwise they tend to be a bit soft.

> 1 quart strawberries, cleaned
> 2 tablespoons sugar

Place whole berries in a bowl and sprinkle sugar over them. Stir gently so sugar coats all the berries. Spoon into airtight freezer bags. Store in freezer. To thaw, place in refrigerator in a covered bowl for 3 to 4 hours. Makes 4 cups.

APPLES

*A*PPLE TREES have come and gone around the farm. Until it was split by lightning, the family favorite was the tree with Pound Sweets—big, sweet, yellow apples Grandma used to pile high in pies. Then there were some McIntosh and a hybrid variety from seed Uncle Mike sent back from California after the war. My father says that these two somehow crossed over to produce another variety, similar to a Snow apple, with a pinkish tinge throughout, that he's never seen anywhere else. These are the ones Grandma baked nonchalantly on the back of the stovetop for a simple winter dessert and the ones the kids brought up from the cellar to munch on for snacks all winter long. Every October the last of the apple crop would be taken to Vernon and pressed into cider. One barrel of this was set aside and raisins added to hasten the fermentation process. Two or three gallons of cider were drained, then the barrel was left outside to freeze. By Christmastime, the applejack—over 90 proof, Dad maintains—would be ready for us to toast family and friends over the holidays, a Depression alternative to expensive liquors.

Dinner Party Spiced Apples

The way Mom and Dad used to do apples for their cookware dinner parties.

> 4 large apples, unpeeled, cored and halved (a firm,
>   tart variety, such as McIntosh or Rome Beauty)
> ½ cup brown sugar
> 2 tablespoons cinnamon candies ("red hots")
> 1 cup water

Place apples, skin side down, in 12-inch skillet. Sprinkle with brown sugar and cinnamon candies. Pour water into bottom of pan. Bring water to boiling point over high heat. Cover skillet and reduce heat until just a small amount of vapor continues to escape. Cook another 20 minutes, or until apples are soft, but not mushy. Serves 4.

Apple Pie

Grandma used the same technique the professionals use to get a light, flaky crust—lard substituted for half the shortening.

Crust:

> 2 cups unbleached flour
> ½ teaspoon salt
> ⅓ cup lard
> ⅓ cup vegetable shortening
> ¼ cup or more cold water

Sift flour and salt into a large mixing bowl. Cut in lard and shortening with a fork or your fingertips until the mixture resembles small beads throughout. Add water, stirring gently, to moisten flour mixture. Add more water, a teaspoonful at a time, until mixture can just be formed into a ball. Divide dough into two parts, one slightly larger than the other. Wrap in plastic wrap and refrigerate while you prepare filling.

Filling:

1 medium-sized apples (a firm, tart variety such as
      McIntosh or Rome Beauty), 5 cups sliced
Juice of one lemon (optional—use only if apples are
      bland)
¼ cup sugar
1 tablespoon cornstarch
1 teaspoon cinnamon
½ teaspoon vanilla extract
⅛ teaspoon nutmeg
1 tablespoon butter

Peel and core apples, then slice ½- to ¾-inch thick (thinner slices become mushy during baking). Combine apples and all other ingredients except butter in a large mixing bowl. Stir gently until apple slices are coated.

To assemble pie, roll out larger dough ball on a lightly floured surface to a thickness of ⅛ inch. To prevent the formation of gluten, which toughens the crust, avoid excessive rolling. Repair tears with a small patch of dough rather than reshaping the ball and rolling out a second time. Transfer dough to ungreased 9-inch pie tin by rolling around rolling pin, then unrolling into place in pan. Trim edges to a 1-inch overhang all around. *Do not pierce bottom crust with fork.*

Spoon filling into shell, making sure the top is well-rounded (it will level off during baking as apples settle). Dot with butter.

Roll out smaller dough ball. Transfer to cover filling and crimp edges with your fingers or a fork to seal them, preventing juices from spilling over during baking. Slit top crust in two or three places with a sharp knife to allow steam to escape. Bake in the middle of the oven at 425° for 10 minutes, then reduce heat to 350° and bake another 45 minutes, or until crust is golden brown and apples are soft (check with a fork through the slit). Makes one 9-inch pie. Serves 8.

Peaches or Pears in Syrup

The best over ice cream, with cottage cheese for a salad, or as an accompaniment to oatmeal on a cold winter morning. Also makes a delicious pie—follow recipe for Apple Pie (above).

> 1 dozen ripe peaches
> 2 cups sugar
> 1 quart water

Place peaches in a large roasting pan and pour boiling water over to loosen skins. Remove immediately from water, peel, cut in half and remove pit. Pack eight halves in a sterilized quart glass jar. Repeat twice. Grandma always added a peach pit to each jar.

In a medium-sized saucepan, dissolve sugar in water and heat to boiling point, stirring occasionally. Pour hot syrup over contents in the three jars, making sure peaches are covered. Follow manufacturer's directions to seal. Makes 3 quarts.

This recipe also works for pears. Substitute an almond for the peach pit for flavoring.

Fruit Cup,
Linda's Way

Use fresh fruit when possible, and don't be afraid to add what's in season.

2 grapefruit and their juice
4 oranges and their juice
12 ounces pineapple, approximately 1 cup
1 apple, peeled
4 peaches, peeled and sliced
2 dozen purple grapes, halved and seeds removed
1 banana, sliced
10 maraschino cherries and ¼ cup packing juice
Orange juice
Sugar or honey (optional)

Remove grapefruit and orange sections from the rinds. Cut pineapple and apple into spoon-size chunks. Combine all fruits in a large serving bowl and add enough orange juice to cover. Add sugar or honey if desired. Serves 8 to 10.

Bananas for Breakfast

1 banana, peeled and sliced into rounds
⅛ teaspoon nutmeg
⅛ teaspoon cinnamon
½ teaspoon honey (optional, depending on ripeness
    of banana)
½ cup milk or half-and-half

Place banana slices in individual serving bowl. Sprinkle with nutmeg and cinnamon. Add honey, if needed. Pour on milk. Serves 1.

Bananas for Company

8 dried figs, sliced in round halves
4 just-ripe bananas, peeled and halved lengthwise
Juice of one lemon
½ cup pineapple juice
Vanilla ice cream

Butter a small, shallow baking dish (8″ × 8″ works well) and arrange fig halves in it, skin side down. Lay banana halves over the figs and squeeze lemon juice over them. Add pineapple juice. Cover dish with foil and bake in 375° oven for 20 minutes. Remove foil and bake another 10 minutes. Serve warm over ice cream. Serves 6 to 8.

Camille's Banana Bread

A favorite after-school snack of her boys, Matt and Greg.

⅓ cup vegetable shortening or butter
⅔ cup sugar
2 eggs, beaten
1¾ cups unbleached flour
2 teaspoons baking powder
¼ teaspoon baking soda
½ teaspoon salt
1 cup mashed bananas (Camille says the browner the better)
½ cup walnuts, chopped fine

In large mixing bowl, beat shortening, sugar and eggs until creamy. In a separate bowl, sift together flour, baking powder, baking soda and salt. Add to creamed mixture in increments, alternating with the mashed banana. Beat well after each addition. Fold in nutmeats. Pour into greased 9″ × 5″ × 3″ loaf pan and bake in the middle of the oven at 350° for one hour. Cool 10 minutes in the pan before attempting to turn out. The bread will crumble less if allowed to rest overnight before slicing, but, really, children don't care about the crumbs! Makes 1 loaf.

Camille's Cranberry Bread

A festive addition to the Thanksgiving or Christmas table. Not too sweet, either, and the fruit doesn't have to be chopped or precooked.

2 cups unbleached flour
½ teaspoon salt
1½ teaspoons baking powder
½ teaspoon baking soda
1 cup sugar
1 egg, beaten
2 tablespoons melted butter, vegetable shortening or
    corn oil
½ cup orange juice
2 tablespoons hot water
½ cup chopped walnuts
1 cup fresh cranberries

In a large mixing bowl, sift the flour, salt, baking powder, baking soda, and sugar. In another bowl, combine the egg, shortening, orange juice and hot water. Pour into flour mixture and stir until moistened. Fold in nuts and berries. Pour into a greased loaf pan (4″ × 8″) and bake in the middle of the oven at 325° for 70 minutes. Makes 1 loaf.

Dried Figs Stuffed with Almonds

An Old Country way with the green figs Grandma used to buy from the Italian importer. Making these reminded her of feast days in her girlhood when stuffed figs were a special confection. Of course, in Italy fresh, soft figs were available most of the time right off the trees.

> 1 pound fresh, green figs (ask at your Italian specialty store when some will be available)
> Whole almonds

Cut figs into round halves and insert a whole almond into each. Press halves together. Place on wire rack and dry in 140° oven for an hour, then open oven door, leaving the oven setting at 140°, and dry another two hours, or until figs are as dry as you like them. Store in a heavy plastic, airtight bag or in a tin with a tight lid. Makes 1 pound.

Chestnuts

Sitting around the table late in the afternoon shelling chestnuts is one of our family "musts" at Thanksgiving and Christmas. Be careful not to burn your fingers or mouth on the boiled ones by misjudging how hot they are right out of the water. After you have their shells off, let chestnuts sit for a few minutes before trying to eat them. A glass of sweet wine with these makes a connoisseur's dessert.

To boil, place chestnuts in a large kettle and cover with water. Bring to a boil, cover, and simmer for one hour. To test for doneness, remove one, peel it and taste. It should be tender, faintly sweet, and pearly in color. Drain, and serve. One pound will serve three or four people. Each person peels his or her own.

To roast, use a very strong, sharp knife to slit a crosshatch through the flat side of the shell of each nut. Arrange in a single layer on an ungreased cookie sheet and bake at 375° for 40 minutes or until tender.

Grape Juice

My mother and Jeannie Chmielewski, our neighbor across the road who lives in the old Graziano family home (her husband, John, is a Graziano grandson), make a grape juice out of Jeannie's own grapes that sparkles at breakfast. The kids are also fond of it at other meals as it's much less concentrated and more fruity-tasting than commercial varieties.

> 1 bushel blue Concord grapes
> Water
> Sugar, as needed

Rinse and drain grapes. Remove fruit from stems and place half the total amount in a large (14-quart or larger) canning kettle that you've filled with water to a depth of two inches. Cover kettle and bring water to boil over medium high heat. As bottom layer of grapes begins to warm and release juice, turn contents to allow upper layers to warm. Lower to a simmer and re-cover. Repeat the grape turning procedure three or four times in the next 45 minutes. When the entire mixture is hot and a great deal of juice has been released, remove the kettle from the heat. Strain the grape pulp and juice, a quart at a time, through fine cheesecloth into another large kettle. Press the pulp with the back of a serving spoon or ladle to obtain all the juice. Repeat entire process with second half of the washed grapes.

Taste cooled juice and add sugar gradually, as needed, stirring well after each addition to insure that sugar is completely dissolved. Ladle juice into one-quart glass canning jars, seal according to manufacturer's directions, and place in hot water canning bath (see directions for Canned Tomatoes, p. 82) for 30 minutes. Cool to room temperature. Store in a cool, dark place to preserve color. Refrigerate two hours before serving. Makes 20 to 22 quarts.

Lemonade

Why settle for something that's advertised as having only the *taste* of good old-fashioned lemonade, when good old-fashioned lemons are so easy to come by? A glass of this was Grandma's answer to a parched throat from picking strawberries or just running around with my cousins on a Sunday afternoon. Lemons were one of the few fruits Grandma was willing to purchase. On reunion day, we can hardly keep the pitchers full!

Ice cubes
Juice of 10 lemons
6 cups cold water
½ cup or more sugar (superfine dissolves quicker)

Into a 2-quart pitcher, add ice cubes until pitcher is half full. Roll lemons back and forth on the counter, pressing with your hand all the while, to release juice before you cut them open. Cut and squeeze, or twist on individual juicer. Discard seeds, but add pulp to the pitcher along with the juice. Stir in water and sugar until all sugar is dissolved. The amount of sugar needed will vary depending on your taste and the amount of juice in the lemons. We like ours on the tart side. Makes 8 glasses.

Hot Lemonade

Feels oh-so-good to a sore throat in the middle of winter and provides vitamin C to help get rid of your cold.

Juice of 5 lemons
3 cups boiling water
¼ cup clover honey

In a small saucepan, combine ingredients and stir well until honey is dissolved. Serve hot. Makes 4 cups.

Choosing from
the pastry shop window

7

Desserts & Coffee

THE REUNION draws to a close in the same way that all those Sunday afternoons at Grandma's did: with a dazzling array of cakes and pastries, some made at home, some brought from the Italian bakeries of East Utica, and always accompanied by pots and pots of dark, strong coffee. By this time of day, the children are back from a walk up the road. The arguments of the day have been settled. Even the winner of the marathon poker game has pretty much been decided, although the men continue to lay down each card with elaborate gestures until the last one has been revealed.

You'd think the outcome of the entire game depended on the turn of each card, the way they grip the one they're about to play for all they're worth, raise it as though against an incredibly heavy weight with a full arm motion as high as their forehead, then suddenly slap it down with a snap of the wrist, a grimace, and an energized grunt—for all the world like administering the coup de grace to a vanquished opponent. My grandfather and his cronies went on like this for hours. My father and his friends play this way, too, but I've yet to see a non-Italian (even one who's been in the family for years by marriage) master the art.

These pastries, served with beer or wine, make strenuous Italian card-playing possible!

Barese Pepper Pastry

5 cups pastry flour
¾ cup olive oil
1 teaspoon salt
1¼ teaspoons freshly ground black pepper
1 teaspoon anise seed
¼ cup or more dry white wine

In a large mixing bowl, combine all ingredients to make a medium soft dough. Knead on a floured surface until smooth. Let rest for 15 minutes with a damp towel over the top of the dough ball to prevent it from drying out and forming a crust. Roll out with your hands into pencil-shaped strips and form into rings 1½ inches in diameter. Place rings on ungreased cookie sheet and bake in the middle of the oven at 400° until very lightly browned. They should be crunchy. Cool before serving. Makes 5 dozen.

Cinnamon Buns

All Saturday afternoon when she was a teenager, Aunt Esther made these in preparation for the Sunday onslaught of company. She remembers Grandma's rule: none for the kids to eat until the company arrived!

Pastry:

½ cup sugar
¼ teaspoon salt
½ cup butter
2 eggs, slightly beaten
3 cups unbleached flour
4 teaspoons baking powder
1 cup milk
1 teaspoon vanilla extract
½ cup raisins

In a large mixing bowl cream sugar, salt and butter. Add eggs and combine well. Sift flour and baking powder into another bowl, then add to egg mixture. Stir well. Add milk, vanilla, and raisins, stirring until mixture is thoroughly moistened and dough handles easily.

Turn out on a floured surface and knead until smooth, adding a bit of flour, as needed, to prevent dough from sticking. Divide dough into halves. Roll out each into an oblong ¼-inch thick.

Filling:

1 cup sugar
2 teaspoons cinnamon
6 tablespoons butter, softened to room temperature

Combine ingredients in a small mixing bowl. Divide into two parts and scatter one half onto first oblong of dough. Roll dough into the shape of a jellyroll, starting with a long side, and cut with a sharp knife into ½-inch-thick slices. Repeat with second half of filling mixture and second piece of dough.

Lay slices close together on greased or oiled baking sheet (10″ × 15″). They will rise during baking to touch one another. Bake at 350° in the middle of the oven for 30 minutes or until light brown and firm. Remove from oven and let cool on a wire rack while you prepare icing.

Icing:

1 cup confectioners' sugar
1 teaspoon almond or vanilla extract
¼ cup milk

Combine ingredients in a small mixing bowl. Spread over slightly warm buns and serve, split, with butter. Makes 18 buns.

Italian Sponge Cake

Grandma served this with crushed, sweetened straw-berries for topping, but any fresh fruit may be used.

6 egg whites, at room temperature
6 egg yolks, at room temperature
1 cup sugar, sifted
1½ teaspoons vanilla *or*
1 tablespoon lemon juice and rind of ½ lemon,
    grated *or*
1 teaspoon orange juice concentrate and 1 teaspoon
    grated orange rind *or,*
6 drops anise extract
¼ teaspoon salt
1½ cups unbleached flour, sifted
1½ teaspoons baking powder (optional)

Separate eggs into two large mixing bowls. Using electric mixer (or whisk, if you're feeling especially vigorous!), beat yolks with sugar until smooth and frothy (about five minutes). Add the flavoring of your choice and the salt, stirring until well combined. If you use baking powder (an insurance that the cake will rise and stay there), sift it with the flour into a third bowl, then add in increments to the yolk mixture, stirring well after each addition so batter becomes very smooth.

Beat egg whites until stiff but not dry. They should form a peak that just barely droops on top when you remove the beaters. Fold beaten egg whites gently into the yolk mixture (this is what provides the lift to the batter even if you don't use baking powder) using a flat serving spoon or spatula. Be sure to incorporate batter from the bottom of the bowl so the finished mixture is of uniform color and consistency.

Scrub a 10-inch tube pan and scald with boiling water. Any oil or grease adhering to the pan will prevent the cake from rising. Cool the pan to room temperature, then fill with the batter, trying not to layer the batter on itself (a way of preventing undesirable air pockets). Bake on the bottom rack of a 350° oven for 45 minutes or until a very sharp knife inserted into the center comes out clean and the top is lightly toasted.

To cool, suspend upside down on a metal funnel or a large soda bottle for *at least* 1½ hours. When the pan is no longer warm to the touch, run a sharp knife around the outside edge and gently slide it up and down around the inside tube edge to break any small section of batter clinging to the sides of the pan (by this time, the sides of the cake have usually retracted away from the sides of the pan). Gently jiggle the pan while holding it upside down and close to the counter top. This loosens the bottom of the cake from the pan and the whole cake should drop out. Place on plate right side up. To cut, use a cake divider or pull apart with fingers. Some people with a gentle touch are able to use a serrated edge bread knife, drawing it back and forth very lightly so as not to crush the edges of the cake. Serve on individual plates with fresh, crushed fruit spooned over. To gild the lily, pass whipped cream. Serves 8.

Pastaciotta Florentine

Oh, how we wheedled dimes out of my mother to run over to Bleecker Street and buy these fluted-side tarts with their sturdy, tender crust, their dense sweet filling, their hint-of-chocolate fragrance—a Friday (pay day) rapture! We'd tag along with Mom when she went to settle the week's accounts at George's Grocery on the corner, and if there were three dimes left in her purse, we were off. The old-fashioned café seemed slightly forbidding, what with all the old men sitting in wrought iron chairs, nursing demitasses of espresso and acting as if it was their private club, but the reward for our bravery was well worth the self-conscious walk past the tables back to the dark wood display counters in the rear of the shop. There the pastaciotta nestled on sparkling glass, lace paper-lined shelves. Some were filled with vanilla, but our passion was only for the chocolate.

If we arrived at just the right time, the pastries would be still warm, their pudding-like centers mingling with the shell. Later in the day, after being refrigerated, the chilled filling stayed more to itself and the crust firmed up so the tastes were slightly more distinct. I was never able to decide which way was best, so I imagined a day sometime in the far future when I'd be rich enough to buy two for myself, one to eat warm, the other to take home and eat chilled later. Of all the desserts we ever had as children, pastaciotta were our undisputed first choice. Even today, when my sisters hear of people about to go to Utica, they ask if they're going anywhere near the bakery so they could bring back some pastaciotta!

Louis D'Amico, the proprietor of the bakery in the 1950s, died, taking with him all of his master pastry recipes. Today, we buy from Gabe Alessandroni of the Florentine Pastry Shop, current holder of the accolade, "the best pastaciotta in town." Many people make these at home, but in reviewing their recipes, I find two major differences from the way Gabe does it: they generally use vegetable shortening and brown sugar, he prefers lard and honey. His product is much softer and more moist—exactly as I remember it from the Fridays of my childhood. This is how to do it à la Florentine.

Pastry:

6 ounces lard
1⅛ cups sugar
5 teaspoons honey
⅓ cup water
2½ cups pastry flour
1½ cups unbleached flour
3 teaspoons baking powder

In a large mixing bowl, cream lard and sugar. Add honey and water, stirring until mixture is smooth. Add flours and baking powder, a bit at a time, until a stiff dough ball forms. Turn out onto a lightly floured surface, form into a sausage-shaped roll with your hands, wrap in plastic wrap, and refrigerate. Remove from refrigerator one hour before you plan to roll out the dough. Refrigerating it contributes to a flakier texture in the finished crust.

Filling:

Crema Pasticceria

1 quart whole milk
1¾ cups sugar
1 cup pastry flour
⅔ cup cocoa (*not* cocoa mix)
6 egg yolks, beaten
½ teaspoon vanilla extract

In a medium-sized, heavy saucepan bring milk to the boiling point. Meanwhile, combine sugar, flour and cocoa in a mixing bowl. Add egg yolks and vanilla to cocoa mixture, stirring until dry ingredients are well moistened and no lumps remain. Add one cup of the hot milk to the cocoa mixture and mix well. Pour the cocoa mixture into the hot milk remaining in the saucepan. Bring mixture to the boiling point again over low heat, stirring continuously to prevent scorching. Filling will begin to thicken and bubble. Immediately raise heat to high and boil furiously 10 to 15 seconds while stirring vigorously. Remove from heat at once, turn out into a large bowl, and cool to room temperature. To prevent a crust from forming, spread a thin layer of butter over the surface of the pudding.

To assemble pastaciotta, divide dough ball into thirds. Use two of the thirds to form 18 balls. Roll out each ball on a lightly floured surface to a thickness of ¼ inch. Press into greased and floured pastaciotta tins (approximately 4 inches in diameter with a characteristic fluted side), leaving ¼-inch overhang all around. Fill. Roll out remaining third of dough to a thickness of ¼ inch and cut out circles of dough to fit tops of tart tins. Press edges of top and sides together to seal, and trim away excess dough. Bake 12 to 15 minutes at 450° or until dark brown (the honey makes a darker crust). Cool. Remove from pans. Serve at once at room temperature, or chill. Store in refrigerator, boxed or wrapped in plastic wrap. Makes 18 pastaciotta.

Note: Nothing but pastaciotta tins will do in making this recipe. Standard tart pans are too shallow, muffin tins are too deep and not wide enough in diameter, individual quiche dishes are too large. The pastaciotta tins can be used for other kinds of tarts, so they are not quite such an extravagance to add to your kitchen equipment. They may be ordered from:

N. J. Flihan and Co.
747 Bleecker Street
Utica, New York 13501

Cannoli Florentine

It's been said of my grandfather that the Baptismal parties he threw in honor of his newborn children gave him the most pleasure of all the family get-togethers. He was a proud papa who issued invitations to friends and relatives far and wide for a big spread that included fancy desserts in addition to beer, peanuts, cold cuts of all sorts and the best the farm had to offer in the way of meats, vegetables, fruits, and, of course, his own excellent wine. On such special occasions he would even bring out his vintage concertina and serenade the crowd or play the tarantella for dancing, giving the person cranking the Victrola a break. His voice couldn't compare to that of Caruso on their beloved opera recordings, but under these circumstances I'm sure Grandpa brought down the house!

In those days, Baptism was no mere formality. Great care was taken in the selection of a godmother and godfather for the baby since they were pledged to see to the child's upbringing should something happen to the parents. This, unfortunately, occurred often enough to make people take their commitments seriously. Their private, personal nature bound family to family, strengthening the community with sacred promises of mutual aid in times of trouble. And it was one more reason why, when I was a child, it was hard to walk down certain streets in East Utica without meeting at least ten people who knew exactly who you were, even if you couldn't quite place them.

One way that these ties were celebrated was with a tray of cannoli from the Florentine Pastry Shop, the highlight of the table of sweets at Grandma and Grandpa's Baptismal parties.

Pastry:

2 tablespoons lard
⅓ cup confectioners' sugar
⅛ teaspoon salt
3 egg yolks
1 whole egg
4 ounces dry white wine
1 tablespoon olive oil
2½ cups pastry flour
1½ cups unbleached flour
1 egg white, slightly beaten
Lard for deep-frying
Confectioners' sugar

Cream lard and sugar in a large mixing bowl. Add salt. In a separate bowl, combine egg yolks, whole egg, wine, and olive oil. Stir liquid mixture into sugar mixture. Sift the flours together in a third bowl, then stir into liquid mixture. Combine thoroughly. Brush on a thin coating of olive oil to prevent a crust from forming, then cover bowl and refrigerate for one hour.

Turn out on a lightly floured surface and form into a sausage-shaped roll with your hands. Cut the roll into rounds approximately ½-inch thick, weighing slightly under one ounce. With a rolling pin, shape each round into an oval no thicker than ⅛ inch. Wrap dough *loosely* around cannoli forms (aluminum tubes or wooden sticks, 6″ × ¾″). The pastry puffs as it cooks, so don't worry if yours is very thin as you wrap it. You want the shells to be crunchy and flaky, not thick and chewy. Seal edges of dough with egg white. Have a complete batch of forms wrapped before you begin to deep-fry as the process moves speedily.

In a deep saucepan or electric deep-fryer, heat lard to 360°.

It should be deep enough to permit cannoli forms to float without touching the bottom of the pan. Fry only as many pastries at one time as can float without touching one another. Overcrowding makes it likely that some pastries will be unevenly cooked—an unnecessary disappointment. Turn pastries several times as they fry so they brown evenly. Remove from deep fryer with tongs when pastries are golden brown. Drain on paper towelling. After the cannoli shells have cooled for approximately 5 minutes, gently push the forms through and out of the shells to assist with cooling all the way through. *Do not attempt to fill the shells until they are completely cooled.*

Filling:

1 pound pastry ricotta (*see* below)
1 tablespoon vanilla extract *or*
1 tablespoon lemon extract
1¼ cups granulated sugar
4 ounces semisweet chocolate, finely shaved
    (optional)

Pastry ricotta is much drier than regular. To use regular ricotta in this recipe, place in a fine cheesecloth bag or in a very fine sieve and let drain at least three hours before combining with other ingredients. In a medium-sized bowl, add vanilla or lemon extract and sugar to ricotta, stirring gently until well combined. If desired, add chocolate curls to vanilla-flavored ricotta. It will color the entire filling to a light brown tone. Some people also add candied fruits, but we prefer to let the flavor of the ricotta stand out. Fill cannoli shells by spooning ricotta mixture inside (a long-handled iced tea spoon is very helpful, but a table knife also works well). Sprinkle lightly with powdered sugar. Makes 18 cannoli.

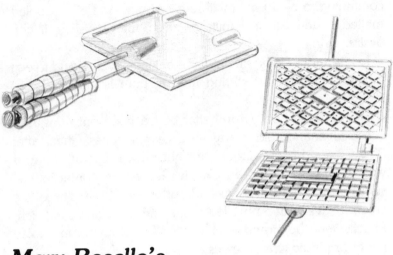

Mary Rosello's Pizzelle

Another special dessert for parties. Especially festive with homemade ice cream. Pizzelle irons may be purchased at Italian stores or in the kitchenware departments of large department stores.

> 6 medium eggs
> 1½ cups sugar
> ⅞ cup corn oil or 1 cup butter, melted
> 2 teaspoons vanilla *or*
> 10 drops anise extract
> 1 tablespoon rye whiskey (optional—use only in
>   combination with the vanilla flavoring)
> 3½ cups unbleached flour
> 4 teaspoons baking powder
> Confectioners' sugar (optional)

In a large mixing bowl, beat eggs. Add sugar gradually, continuing to beat until mixture is smooth. Add oil or cooled melted butter. Stir in vanilla or anise, then whiskey, if you desire.

In a separate bowl, sift flour and baking powder. Add to egg mixture, folding and stirring until mixture is very wet and sticky.

Heat pizzelle iron. Drop batter by teaspoon onto hot iron. Close cover and hold steady while steam escapes. Check after 30 seconds. Pizzelle should be light brown. Lift off the iron with a fork, and cool on a rack. Serve with confectioners' sugar dusted over, with melted butter, or with a slice of ice cream between two pizzelle to make an ice cream sandwich. Pizzelle may be stored after cooling by wrapping in waxed paper or plastic wrap. Serves 8.

Gelati Florentine

Aunt Tessie and Uncle Aioley bring their ice cream maker to Mom's a few times over the summer, incorporating whatever fruit is in season into the rich, cold treat. This recipe for Italian ice cream made from an egg custard is a classic from the Florentine Pastry Shop that can be varied many ways—all delicious!

    6 egg yolks
    1½ cups sugar
    1 quart whole milk
    2 strips lemon peel
    2 tablespoons vanilla extract

In a large mixing bowl, beat egg yolks and sugar until mixture becomes fluffy (at least 10 minutes). Add milk, vanilla extract, and lemon peel, stirring until sugar is completely dissolved. Pour mixture into the top portion of a double boiler and cook over very low heat until it thickens somewhat to the consistency of light cream. Stir continuously to prevent lumps from forming. Pour thickened mixture through very fine strainer and cool in the refrigerator. When thoroughly chilled, spoon into an ice cream machine (either electric or hand-turned) and dash until mixture solidifies. Makes a bit over one quart. If you want to be able to slice this ice cream, freeze another two hours in an airtight freezer bag lining a box or tin that's the shape you need.

To vary:

RECIPE VARIATIONS

Flavor	Modifications of Basic Recipe
CHOCOLATE	Substitute 6 ounces cocoa for lemon peel before putting mixture into double boiler.
MAPLE WALNUT	Substitute brown sugar for white and add ⅔ cup chopped walnuts halfway through the time required with your ice cream machine.
CHERRY VANILLA	Add 1 cup maraschino cherries halfway through the time required with your ice cream machine.
BUTTER PECAN	Add ⅔ cup chopped pecans and ⅓ cup butterscotch chips halfway through the time required with your ice cream machine.

Flavor	Modifications of Basic Recipe
STRAWBERRY	Add ⅔ cup strawberry preserves or jam and ⅔ cup sliced fresh strawberries halfway through the time required with your ice cream machine.
PEACH	Add ⅔ cup peach preserves and ⅔ cup chopped fresh peaches halfway through the time required with your ice cream machine.
CHOCOLATE MINT	Add ¼ cup crème de menthe to the mixture before placing in double boiler. Add ⅔ cup chocolate chips halfway through the time required with your ice cream machine.
RUM RAISIN	Add ¼ cup white rum to the mixture before placing in double boiler. Add ⅔ cup prefrozen raisins halfway through the time required with your ice cream machine.

Porchide (Pignolata or Strufoli)

Grandma made these little, honey-coated beads arranged in a mound in a fancy bowl every Christmas, along with her peanut cookies and fig cookies. Neapolitans call this dessert *strufoli*. If you add pignolia nuts to the recipe, you have *pignolata*. But to people from Apulia, they're *porchide* (little pigs) because they puff up as they deep-fry until they look like a pile of piglets!

> 2½ cups unbleached flour
> 1 teaspoon baking powder
> ½ teaspoon salt
> 1½ tablespoons white wine
> 3 cups corn oil
> 3 eggs, beaten
> ½ cup pignolia nuts (optional)
> 1¼ cups honey
> Multicolored candy sprinkles

On a pastry board or in a large mixing bowl, combine flour, baking powder and salt. Make a well in the center and fill with the wine, ⅛ cup of oil, and the eggs. Gradually scoop small amounts of flour from the outside edges of the well and move to the center, combining all ingredients with your fingers as you work. After dough is of even texture throughout, knead it on a lightly floured surface for 3 minutes or until smooth, soft and elastic.

Roll out dough to a thickness of ¼ inch. Cut into thin strips, then roll each strip into a pencil shape with your hands. Cut off nuggets ¼-inch long. To form porchide, stretch each nugget slightly over your middle fingertip as you roll it lightly against a hand grater, leaving a dimpled surface. The porchide will be slightly curled in on itself like a conch shell—a factor that makes each nugget puff when frying.

In a deep saucepan or electric deep fryer, bring 2⅞ cups oil to 350°. Drop in a cup or so of nuggets and fry until they rise to the top and are light golden brown. The oil foams a bit while the frying takes place. Remove the porchide with a slotted spoon or strainer and drain on paper towels. Cool. Transfer to a large serving bowl. Add pignolia nuts, if desired.

In a small saucepan, boil honey until it begins to crystallize. Pour over the porchide and stir until all are coated. Shape into a mound and scatter sprinkles over all. Store covered with plastic wrap, unrefrigerated. Makes 5 cups.

Barese Peanut Cookies

Made in all Barese households at Christmastime. It is essential to the special flavor of this recipe to use raw peanuts which you roast yourself.

1 cup raw peanuts, shelled
1¼ cups sugar
1 cup corn oil
Juice and grated rind of one lemon
1¼ teaspoons vanilla
¼ teaspoon ground cloves
6 eggs, beaten
5½ cups unbleached flour
5½ teaspoons baking powder

Roast peanuts in a skillet over medium heat for 10 minutes, shaking pan and stirring nuts to prevent scorching. If peanuts have skins, blow gently over the roasted nuts and the skins will fly away (Grandma used to stand on the back porch to do this). Place roasted nuts in a single layer between sheets of paper towel and crush into very small pieces with a rolling pin.

In a large mixing bowl, combine peanuts with all ingredients except flour and baking powder. Combine flour and baking powder in another bowl, then add, one cup at a time, to the peanut mixture. The dough will become quite stiff and you will be able to form it into a ball without leaving much on the sides of the bowl.

Turn out onto a lightly floured surface and knead five minutes. Dough must become smooth and glossy. Divide dough mass into two pieces, then roll each back and forth with your hands to form two sausage-shaped rolls about 1½ inches in diameter. Flatten the top of the rolls slightly by rolling them gently with a rolling pin. Form diamond-shaped pieces by cutting the dough on the diagonal with a sharp knife.

Lightly grease or oil a cookie sheet. Space cookies ½ inch apart (they don't spread) and bake in the middle of a 400° oven about 8 minutes or until just the palest brown. Avoid overbaking or they will be too hard and dry. Cool 30 minutes, then ice.

Icing:

1½ cups confectioners' sugar
2 tablespoons water
½ teaspoon almond extract
Multicolored candy sprinkles

In a small mixing bowl combine sugar, water and flavoring. Dip tops of cookies into icing and immediately scatter a pinch of sprinkles over each. Icing hardens quickly, holding sprinkles in place. Makes 10 dozen.

Christmas Fig Cookies

Grandma's way with ripe figs.

Filling:

2 cups soft, ripe figs (not dried)
½ cup sugar
1 cup orange juice
½ teaspoon salt

Chop figs very fine and combine with other ingredients in a medium-sized saucepan. Cook over moderate heat for 5 minutes, stirring all the time to achieve a smooth consistency. Remove from heat and cool to room temperature.

Dough:

1 cup butter or shortening
½ cup sugar
½ cup brown sugar
1 egg
¼ cup milk
1 teaspoon vanilla extract
3 cups flour
½ teaspoon salt
½ teaspoon baking soda

In a large mixing bowl, cream butter and sugars. In another small bowl, beat egg, milk and vanilla. Add to butter mixture. Stir well. The sugar should be completely dissolved. In a third bowl, sift flour, salt and soda together. Add gradually to sugar mixture to form a very stiff dough.

On a lightly floured surface, roll out dough to the thickness of a pie crust. Spread cooled filling over the entire surface of the dough, then roll into a jellyroll shape. Wrap in waxed paper or plastic wrap and refrigerate for one hour.

Unwrap, slice into ¼-inch thick rounds and place on ungreased cookie sheet. Leave ½ inch between cookies. Bake for 10 minutes in a 375° oven. Cool. Store in covered container at room temperature or slightly below. Makes 5 or 6 dozen.

Pola Cecarelli
Truman's Fruitcake

Mom dislikes heavy, dark, alcohol-laden fruitcake, so when her good friend, Pola Truman, offered her this light version, she tested it right away. The result: a new family favorite. Well, relatively new—Mom's been making it now for about 15 years! To have it for Christmas, make the week after Thanksgiving and freeze in airtight freezer bags until Christmas. Also makes exclaimed-over holiday gifts for neighbors.

½ cup butter
1½ cups sugar
5 eggs
1 cup applesauce
2 cups unbleached flour
⅛ teaspoon salt
1 teaspoon baking powder
½ teaspoon baking soda
1 teaspoon cinnamon
½ teaspoon cloves
1 cup chopped dates
1 cup walnut pieces
½ cup unbleached flour
12 maraschino cherries

In a large mixing bowl, cream butter and sugar, then stir in eggs, one at a time. Fold in applesauce. In another bowl, sift 2 cups flour, salt, baking powder, baking soda, cinnamon and cloves together. In a third bowl, dredge dates and walnut pieces in ½ cup flour.

Gradually stir dry ingredients into applesauce mixture to make a smooth batter. Fold in flour-coated dates and walnuts. Pour into greased or oiled loaf pan or tube pan. Stud top with cherries. Bake in middle of 325° oven for one hour. Serves 12.

Pastry Easter Baskets

One of these for each of the children and a porchful of gardenia plants for Grandma were hallmarks of Easter Sunday at the farm. Grandma kept busy all of the week preceding Easter making the baskets. These days Aunt Esther keeps up the tradition. This recipe will make three baskets, or this amount of dough can also be formed into a large wreath and decorated as a centerpiece for the Easter dinner table. Just remember that Grandma always said it was bad luck to have an even number of eggs encased in the wreath!

Dough:

1 cup milk
4 tablespoons butter or lard
½ cup sugar
3 eggs, beaten
1 tablespoon grated lemon rind
1 tablespoon grated orange rind
½ teaspoon anise seed (optional)
1 yeast cake or 2 packages dry yeast
¼ cup warm water
½ teaspoon sugar
3 cups unbleached flour
3 hard-boiled eggs, in their shells

In a small saucepan, heat milk, butter, and sugar over medium heat, stirring until butter melts and sugar dissolves. Pour mixture into large mixing bowl. Cool to room temperature, then stir in beaten eggs and flavorings.

Dissolve yeast in warm water, adding ½ teaspoon sugar to "proof" the yeast. If no bubbles or foam begin to appear on the surface of the yeast mixture after three minutes, discard and start over with fresh yeast. Add dissolved yeast mixture to milk mixture, stirring thoroughly.

Add flour to liquid ingredients in small amounts, stirring well after each addition, until dough comes away from the sides of the bowl. Turn out on a lightly floured surface and knead until smooth and glossy (approximately 10 minutes). Return dough to oiled pan, cover with damp towel, and let rise until doubled in bulk. Punch down.

Divide dough into thirds, reserving a handful of each third to form a handle and decorations for each basket. Press a hard-boiled egg in shell into the center of each dough mass. Cover it with surrounding dough, smoothing the top. To decorate the top, fashion a cross, flower or bird from the dough and lay on top of the dough covering the egg. Form pencil-shaped strips and braid them to form a handle. Add to the top by pressing its ends into the sides of the basket. Place on a greased or oiled cookie sheet and bake in the middle of a 350° oven for 30 to 40 minutes or until very light brown. Cool. Decorate with icing in colors of your own choosing. Makes 3. Alternatively, form into one large ring and use as a centerpiece for Easter dinner.

Icing:

1 cup confectioners' sugar
2 tablespoons milk
½ teaspoon vanilla extract
Food colorings

Mix in small bowls, keeping colors separate. Apply to decorative elements of baskets with knife or child's paint brush. Icing hardens almost immediately.

Mary Rosello's Ricotta Pie

Another Easter classic, as beautiful and nutritious as can be!

Pastry:

1½ cups unbleached flour, sifted
½ teaspoon salt
½ cup butter or lard
1 egg
¼ cup milk
½ teaspoon vanilla

In a large mixing bowl, sift flour and salt together. Add shortening, cutting it in with a fork until the mixture is of an even, crumbly texture. Stir in egg, milk, and vanilla. Dough should form a ball. Divide dough into two parts, one twice the size of the other. On a lightly floured surface, roll out the larger piece of dough into a circle 11 inches in diameter. Fit it into an oiled and floured 8-inch layer cake pan, leaving a 1-inch overhang all around. Roll out the smaller piece of dough to a thickness of ¼ inch and cut into strips ¼-inch wide.

Filling:

1 pound ricotta cheese
¾ cup sugar
¾ teaspoon salt
5 eggs
¼ pound milk chocolate, coarsely grated

In a large mixing bowl combine ricotta, sugar, salt, and eggs. Beat with an electric mixer on low speed until creamy and smooth. Fold in grated chocolate. Pour into pastry shell. Weave pastry strips to form lattice pattern and place across top of pie. Flute edges and trim away excess crust.

Bake 1½ hours in the middle of a 350° oven or until crust is golden brown. Cool. This pie may be refrigerated successfully (be sure to cover with plastic wrap), but do not freeze as the filling will separate. Serves 8.

Wedding Cheesecake

Tom and I were married in May in a simple ceremony in the garden of our Westchester house. Rhododendrons and baby's breath were in bloom, so Mom helped me arrange them around the base of this cheesecake which we served to our guests. This recipe completely fills a 3-inch deep, 9-inch diameter springform pan. To make a family-sized dessert, use half of all ingredients and a 1½-inch deep, 9-inch diameter cake pan.

Crust:

1 cup very fine graham cracker crumbs
¾ teaspoon cinnamon
6 tablespoons butter, melted
2 tablespoons butter, softened to room temperature

In a medium-sized mixing bowl, combine cracker crumbs with cinnamon. Stir in the melted butter until all crumbs are moistened. Using the softened butter, thickly coat a springform pan or a cake pan, depending on the size of cheesecake you desire. Pour crumb mixture into baking pan, then press evenly against sides and bottom of the pan to make a thin crust. Chill in refrigerator for 30 minutes before filling.

Filling:

24 ounces cream cheese, softened to room
   temperature
1¼ cups sugar
5 egg yolks
1 pint sour cream
3 tablespoons unbleached flour
¼ teaspoon salt
1½ teaspoons vanilla extract
Juice and grated rind of one lemon
5 egg whites

Beat the cream cheese with an electric mixer on low speed until cheese is very soft and smooth. Add sugar, a quarter of a cup at a time, beating until sugar is absorbed. Add yolks, one at a time, then beat in sour cream, flour, salt, vanilla and lemon. Mixture should be of even consistency.

In another bowl, beat egg whites until stiff but not dry. Fold them very gently through the cheese mixture until all is the same color and texture (be sure to incorporate batter from the bottom of the bowl). This step determines how high in the pan your cake will be. Pour the filling mixture into the crust, smoothing it evenly into all sections of the pan. Bake at 325° in the middle of the oven for 1½ hours. Cool for one hour in the turned-off oven with the door open to avoid jiggling it while it's setting. Remove from oven and cool to room temperature. Serve plain, with a sprinkling of confectioners' sugar, or with fruit topping. Serves 20 or 10.

Italian Wedding Cake (Rum Cake Florentine)

In Grandma's bedroom, next to the oak dresser with the votive light to the Virgin, stood the big, black, hobnail-studded steamer trunk from her one and only Atlantic crossing. Inside she kept her hand-knitted and fringed matrimonial bedspread, fine bed and table linens with embroidery, tatting and crochet trims done by her own hand, and stacks of formal family wedding portraits going back to 1920. The brides are, without exception, studies in white, each a stunning example of the height of the milliner's and dress-maker's artistry of their time. There's Cousin Rose Semeraro in white lace, Cousin Mamie in white silk, Cousin Laura in white organza, Carmella Argento in white velvet, Josephine Tramacera in white taffeta, Aunt Annie in white satin, Aunt Millie in pleated white tulle, Aunt Toni in white brocade. But the most beautiful dress of all to me was my mother's—an elegant sweep of lustrous white satin encrusted over the bodice with seed pearls and extending into a near-regal train of rustling ripples. In her hands, the family emblem when it came to wedding bouquets, a mass of creamy white roses and trailing ribbons ordered from the Paradise Flower Shop, run for 50 years by my grandfather's *paesano*, Cosmo Carriero. It is accurate to conclude that no expense was spared on weddings in those days. It was universally expected that one wedding would be it for your entire life, so the feeling was that you'd better have it exactly the way you wanted it—right down to the engraving on the matchbooks!

The indispensable culinary counterpart to the bridal gown and floral bouquet was the three-tiered wedding cake, a sculptured romance of rosettes, garlands, swags, petals, piping, columns, bows and ruffles, a masterpiece of custom baking. Ours invariably came from the Florentine Pastry Shop where today Gabe Alessandroni still decorates each one by hand—including forming each flower petal individually.

Watching him at work on a Saturday morning, the biggest day for weddings, with light streaming in from glass skylights high above slab marble countertops and the atmosphere heavy with the aroma of baking pastry, is like turning the clock back to another era—a time when people really cared about their work and, maybe even more important, *enjoyed* their work. Working with the deft strokes that are the mark of the professional, in 45 minutes he can turn three layers of vanilla cake, a large tub of butter cream frosting, and a few pieces of cardboard and plastic into a cake of such extravagant beauty you wonder if there hasn't been some sort of magic in-volved—even though you've watched every step of the way.

While making such a creation at home is probably far beyond the skills of most of us, there is a return to the traditional in weddings today and many couples (how about those celebrating anniversaries, too?) might love to have a creation made for them by a caterer. Herewith, how to do it, Gabe's way, so that each of 150 people will have a slice.

Cake:

50 medium eggs
4¼ cups granulated sugar (2 pounds)
4 teaspoons vanilla or lemon extract
12 cups pastry flour (3 pounds)
4 tablespoons baking powder (2½ ounces)
2 cups rum (optional)

Crack enough eggs to fill a large mixing bowl one quarter full. Beat at medium high speed with an electric mixer for 12 to 15 minutes until eggs double in volume. Pour beaten eggs into a very large container, such as the top of a turkey roaster, and set aside. Repeat until all eggs are beaten. Add sugar a bit at a time, beating continuously until mixture is smooth (all sugar dissolved). Stir in vanilla or lemon flavoring.

In another large bowl, sift flour and baking powder together, then add gradually to egg mixture, stirring well after each addition until batter is of even consistency throughout.

Grease and dust with flour three 5-inch-deep layer cake pans (diameters: 15 inches, 12 inches, and 9 inches). Pour batter to an even depth in each. Bake at 350° in the middle of the oven approximately 45 minutes, or until the top springs back after you press it gently with your fingertip. Remove cakes from oven and cool on racks, *in the pans,* for 10 minutes. Turn the pans over and gently jiggle until the cakes slip out. Set cakes down on their tops and allow to finish cooling *completely* to room temperature before icing and decorating.

When cool, trim rounded tops with serrated edge knife to make them perfectly flat. Turn layers so trimmed surface is on the bottom. With a pastry brush, saturate the top of each layer with the rum, if you wish. Exercise your judgment about how much rum to use. The cake should remain firm, with only enough rum added to lend a grace note to the whole, not to overpower all the other ingredients. The surface of the layers should never become soggy or sunken under the weight of the rum.

Icing:

Butter Cream Frosting

1 pound (2 cups) butter, softened to room
    temperature
2 pounds (4⅜ cups) vegetable shortening, such as
    Crisco
¼ cup vanilla extract
2¾ pounds (6⅓ cups) confectioners' sugar
3 whites of large eggs
Food coloring (optional)

In a large mixing bowl, beat butter and vegetable shortening together until mixture is of even color. Add vanilla, then sugar, a cup at a time. Beat 5 or 6 minutes with electric mixer on medium speed until sugar is completely absorbed and the mixture is very fluffy. Add egg whites and beat at medium speed for 10 to 15 minutes until the frosting is smooth and glistening. It needs to be stiff enough to hold its shape when formed into decorative elements. If you wish to tint frosting, separate into individual bowls and follow mixing directions on the package of food coloring you are using to obtain the colors you desire.

Assembly and decoration:

The professionals use special equipment to accomplish their architectural effects:

- *white cardboard plates* placed beneath each layer to give support and stability;

- *wooden pegs* just the height of each layer, sunken into the cake to support the layer above;

- *plastic "pillars"* to elevate the top layer with its inscription, floral bouquet and/or figurines;

- *parchment paper or plastic-lined canvas pastry bags* with decorative, interchangeable, *drop-in tips* to fashion the design elements you choose;

- *ruffled lace paper* to border the cardboard base and give it a finished look.

These items, along with hundreds more cake decorating products and a catalog–yearbook that provides a 21-page decorating course are available from:

Wilton Enterprises
2240 W. 85th Street
Woodridge, IL 60515

If you are inexperienced at cake decoration, it will be worth your while to spend an hour or two practicing with your tools to achieve the effects you want. Prepare a small batch of frosting and run your strokes across large pieces of waxed paper. When the batch runs out, scrape the paper clean with a rubber spatula and return the frosting to its container. Repeat as many times as you need to feel confident when you begin to work on the cake. The traditional Florentine Pastry Shop pattern follows, but you may plan and execute any design you like. Another excellent source of ideas: *Creative Cakes* by Stephanie Crookston (New York: Random House, 1978).

Method (Round Cake):

Step	Procedure
1	Trim sides and top of all three layers of cake with serrated edge knife. Brush with rum.
2	*Optional*—Slice each layer in two and fill with pudding, jam, or butter cream frosting.
3	Place 15-inch layer trimmed side down, on cardboard plate with lace paper stapled around outer edge.
4	Insert wooden pegs to support second layer.
5	Place 12-inch layer trimmed side down, on its plate.
6	Center 12-inch layer over bottom layer, making sure cardboard support plate rests evenly on wooden pegs beneath.
7	Using wet knife, smooth a thin layer of butter cream frosting over all.
8	Insert plastic columns to support top layer.
9	Using a fairly small rosette tip in pastry bag, cover line where second layer rests on first with a circlet of rosette blooms.
10	Do the same where the first layer meets the cardboard base plate.
11	Divide bottom layer into evenly-spaced sections and mark each section with a single rosette.
12	Do the same for the second layer, marking the sections with rosettes set midway between those of the bottom layer.
13	Connect the rosettes on the bottom layer with garlands that dip approximately ⅓ the height of the layer.
14	Do the same to the rosettes on the second layer.

Step	Procedure
15	Add a swag under each rosette marking, dropping them just slightly longer than the lowest point of the garlands.
16	Change to a smaller rosette tip, and add baby rosette blooms across the top edge of each garland on both layers. If these are to be a color (to match bridesmaids' gowns, for instance), use a second pastry bag rather than trying to clean and refill the first bag every time you switch colors.
17	Using a third bag and a plain tip, squirt a small dot of contrasting color into the center of each baby rosette bloom.
18	Using a fourth bag with green tinted frosting, add leaves above and below every second baby rosette.
19	Using first bag and a plain tip, add wavy ruffled trim around base and on top of first layer next to band of rosettes (see Step 9).
20	Still using first bag and plain tip, squeeze a circle of frosting at the end of each swag (see Step 15). These will be used to affix large roses.
21	Using bag with green frosting, add leaves to each side of circles (rose will sit over these).
22	Press preformed large roses onto circles.
23	To decorate top of second layer, place one preformed large rose in center, rosettes around bases of pillars, leaves at sides of rosettes and large rose. Arch garlands toward center above each rosette cluster. All should match color scheme established on sides of layers.
24	Place 9-inch layer, trimmed side down, on its plate and attach plate to supporting pillars.

25   Using a wet knife, smooth a thin layer of frosting over top and sides.

26   Using first bag and plain tip, add wavy ruffled trim around circumference of top layer edge.

27   Add circlet of rosettes just inside wavy trim.

28   Add green leaves to rosettes as above.

29   Add garlands as above.

30   Add contrasting centers in rosettes.

31   Place four large preformed roses in center.

32   Place leaves diagonally outward from each rose.

33   Place figurines in center of rose circle.

Note: To preform large roses, stand a large cork from a wine or champagne bottle on its bottom end. Squirt a dollop of frosting onto its top. With an upward lift of the pastry bag and a slightly curved motion, add free-standing "petals," beginning in the center and working outward in rings. By turning the cork from the bottom you need not touch the rose as it's being formed. Lift rose off the cork with a metal spatula, making sure to get the base of the flower as well as the petals. Arrange on waxed paper and refrigerate until needed on cake.

THE WEDDING TRAY

*T*HE HIGHLIGHT of every wedding I can remember attending as a child came toward the end: the band would break into a double-time polka and Uncle Fred (in those days nearly as big around as he was tall) would shout across the room to Aunt Rosie (most pleasingly plump herself), "Hey, Rosie! Let's go!" And before anyone knew what was up, the two of them would be spinning and dipping and kicking up their heels at a furious pace, leaving all the other dancers (the bride and groom included) no choice but to draw back and give them the entire floor.

Both were, as people used to say, "light on their feet," and their dancing was a marvel of coordinated hijinks. Fred would be whooping as he was swooping, and Rosie shook with laughter at being propelled through every top-speed whirl. It was traditional at these weddings to pay cash for the privilege of a dance with the bride, but Fred and Rosie were by far the best act of the day—and they were free. Even the caterer's help would stop in their tracks to take it in, and the applause and cheers at the end were deafening.

As the dancing wound down, the bride and groom began to circulate among the tables, serving guests from a tray heaped with assorted Italian cookies and sugar-coated almonds in white net bags with little cards that said thank you from the wedding couple. A few cookies from the tray were boxed for the bride and groom to take with them on their trip and, clutching the box, they'd make their way through the gauntlet of friends and relatives (Uncles Don, Ray and Bob always positioned themselves in the best possible spots for aiming the pennies, confetti and rice), jump in their car and speed away—off to start another branch of our spreading family tree.

Almond Macaroons (Amaretti)

Aunt Toni and Cousin Grace are the kitchen professionals in our family. Grace teaches cooking classes in Utica and Toni bakes to order. For years, she's started baking for Christmas months ahead of time, her specialty being old-fashioned Italian fancy cookies. These also appear on the wedding tray.

8 ounces almond paste
1 cup sugar
2 egg whites, at room temperature
6 maraschino cherries, cut in quarters

In a large mixing bowl, combine almond paste and sugar, mashing and stirring with a fork. In another bowl, beat egg whites until stiff, but still glistening. Gently fold beaten egg whites into almond mixture, making sure the batter is taken up from the bottom of the bowl and is of even consistency.

Drop batter with pastry tube or teaspoon onto cookie sheet covered with rice paper or brown paper (leftover from shopping bags is fine). The cookies should be 1½ inches in diameter, spaced 1½ inches apart. Decorate each cookie with a quarter of a cherry placed in the center. Let cookies dry, uncovered, on a counter for 3 or 4 hours.

Bake at 325° in the middle of the oven for about 25 minutes, or until very lightly browned. Cool on the baking paper. Makes 2 dozen.

Mostaccioli
(Spice Cookies)

An ancient Apulian sweet, which Grandma had at her wedding. Aunt Esther and Cousin Antoinette make these at Christmastime using Grandma's favorite recipe.

¼ cup sugar
¼ cup vegetable shortening, such as Crisco
2 eggs, slightly beaten
¼ teaspoon cinnamon
¼ teaspoon ground cloves
2 cups unbleached flour
½ teaspoon baking soda
2 teaspoons baking powder
½ cup cocoa
½ cup chopped walnuts or almonds
½ cup milk (approximately)

In a large mixing bowl, cream sugar and shortening together. Stir in eggs until mixture is of even texture. In a separate bowl, sift together cinnamon, cloves, flour, soda, baking powder, and cocoa. Add to egg mixture along with nuts and mix well. Add milk gradually until dough is moist and workable. It should come away from the sides of the bowl cleanly. The exact amount needed will depend on the amount of moisture in the flour.

Turn the dough out on a floured surface and knead until it is glossy and smooth. Form the dough into walnut-sized balls and place them ½ inch apart on a greased or oiled cookie sheet. Bake at 375° for 30 minutes, or until very firm. Cool. Roll in confectioners' sugar before serving or spread thinly with hard icing (see p. 180).

Anise Biscuits Florentine

Easy—and delicious with late-Sunday-morning coffee.

3 eggs
1 cup sugar
1 tablespoon honey
½ teaspoon vanilla extract
½ teaspoon anise extract
2 cups pastry flour
1 teaspoon baking powder

In a large mixing bowl, beat eggs, sugar, honey, vanilla, and anise until fluffy. Stir in flour and baking powder. The batter will be quite thick, but not quite a dough.

Spoon batter into two greased or oiled loaf pans (9″ × 5″ × 3″). Brush flour lightly over the top, using a damp pastry brush.

Bake 10 minutes at 425° or until golden brown. Turn out on a wire rack to cool. When you can handle them comfortably, slice loaves into oblongs 1 inch wide and 5 inches long. Place biscuits on cookie sheet and toast in the middle of 375° oven for another 5 minutes. Makes 18 biscuits.

Cenci (Bow Knots)

On reunion day, these are the pastries the children wait all day for!

1½ cups pastry flour, sifted
¼ teaspoon baking powder
½ teaspoon salt
1 tablespoon sugar
2 tablespoons butter
2 eggs, slightly beaten
2 tablespoons white rum *or*
2 tablespoons white wine and rind of ½ lemon,
    grated
Oil or lard for deep frying
Confectioners' sugar

Sift flour, baking powder, salt, and sugar into a medium-sized mixing bowl. Cut in the butter with a fork until the mixture is even-grained. Stir in eggs and flavoring until mixture is even-colored. The dough will be rather stiff, but pliable.

Turn out onto a lightly floured surface and knead for 10 minutes. Wrap and refrigerate for 1 hour.

Divide dough into four pieces. Roll each piece out to a thickness of ⅛ inch and an 8″ × 10″ shape. Cut into strips ¾-inch wide and 8 inches long. Handling strips gently, form each into a looped, loose knot. Fry three or four at a time in approximately 4 inches of hot oil or lard (350°) until golden and puffy (approximately one or two minutes). Remove with tongs or a slotted spoon and place on paper towels to drain and cool. To serve, sprinkle with confectioners' sugar and pile on a pretty serving platter. Makes 4 dozen.

COFFEE

I HAVE a passion for the aroma of freshly-roasted, freshly-ground coffee beans. As a result of writing this book, I realize that this, too, is an artifact of my childhood: The smell of coffee is indelibly fixed in my memory in association with all the early morning summer breakfasts with Grandpa and late Sunday afternoon dessert sessions at the farm. Coffee from fresh beans was the only kind Grandma ever made.

She was so particular about coffee (or, rather, *Grandpa* was so particular about it—she actually preferred tea!) that she bought green coffee beans, roasted them at home in her cavernous oven until they were very dark brown, then crushed them fine by rolling them with a bottle on the top of the kitchen table. She did this in small batches and her coffee was always remarkable—robust, strong, a pleasure to the eye and the palate. Taken black, it complemented the heavy sweetness of the fancier pastries and baked goods. But served with cream (also fresh from the family cows), concentrated in a demitasse, or teamed with chocolate or spices, it could stand by itself as the end of a meal.

Grandma broke all of today's rules by using a percolator that made coffee with a lot of sediment in it—a very thick brew compared to today's emphasis on a clarified cup—but she never boiled the coffee and perked it only eight minutes so it retained a balanced taste, never bitter. As a child, I found the percolator cheery, its burblings a charming counterpoint to the animated conversation of my aunts as they did the dinner dishes and set the dessert table. Year in and year out we've wound up our family gatherings with pot after pot—and reunion day is no exception.

For best results you'll need:

- double-roasted espresso coffee (fresh-ground or, better yet, the fresh beans themselves which you can grind at home to suit your own taste and the requirements of your coffee pot);
- a coffee grinder (hand-turned or electric);
- a coffee pot (two Italian favorites are the *napoletana* and the *moka,* both of which brew coffee very quickly, but unless made of stainless steel can give a metallic taste to the finished product; the Melitta filter system, conventional drip, and vacuum pots also work beautifully because they prevent the brewed coffee from staying in contact with the spent grounds and prevent it from being forced repeatedly through the grounds as happens in a percolator).

Following a few basic principles will ensure the quality of every cup you brew. First of all, in addition to good, fresh coffee beans, good coffee requires good water. If you don't like the taste of your tap water, you probably won't like the coffee you make with it either, no matter what quality of coffee beans you use. Like many other people, we've solved this problem by installing a charcoal filtering system in our kitchen faucet to purify the water. Ours even removes the chlorine, which, depending on its concentration in the water, can add a harsh flavor.

Second, as coffee brews, oils are released from the grounds. This filmy residue can build up almost invisibly in your pot, making subsequent brewings very bitter. After each use, scrub your pot meticulously with detergent, then baking soda, and rinse well so you start fresh each time.

Finally, because some coffee pots are sold without directions for use, or with directions that are so vague it's impossible to tell when your coffee's ready, you will need to experiment with your pot and the grind of the coffee you're using to achieve the taste you prefer. If you buy several different types of coffee beans, you may want to make a little chart listing the variety and the brewing time for each one to save time and costly mistakes once you hit upon the right combination for each blend. In general, the finer the grind, the shorter the brewing time. This rule, from Joel, David, and Karl Schapira's *The Book of Coffee and Tea* (New York: St. Martin's Press, 1975) applies when water heated to a correct temperature of 200°-205° meets the coffee:

Grind	Brewing Time
Fine	1 to 4 minutes
Drip	4 to 6 minutes
Regular	6 to 8 minutes

Exceeding these time limits means risking a bitter brew.

Dessert Demitasse

Just what you need to cut the sweetness of cannoli or cheesecake. And what a great reason to bring out the dainty demitasse set the kids are always asking to play with! I use a Melitta filter pot for this.

8 coffee measures (16 tablespoons) dark roast Italian
      coffee, finely ground
3 cups cold water

Bring water to full boil in any saucepan. Insert filter into top of your coffee server. Spoon in coffee. Pour boiling water over coffee to begin filtering process, then gradually pour in remaining water until all has passed through to the server. Serve at once. Makes 8 demitasse cups.

Espresso

Technically, you have to have an espresso maker to force steam and boiling water through the coffee (only Italian dark roast, very finely ground, will do), and more of these machines are now being sold in the United States than ever before (check the kitchenware section of your local department store, or see the Directory). Follow the manufacturer's direction carefully as each brand works in a slightly different manner. If you'd rather not invest in an espresso machine, a Melitta filter can be used to approximate true espresso. Follow the recipe above for demitasse, using the darkest roast finely ground. Espresso is served without cream. Instead try a twist of lemon peel and sugar. *Optional:* Dampen edge of espresso cup before pouring in coffee. Dip edge of cup in granulated sugar and allow sugar to harden. Add coffee carefully so as not to disturb the edging. Twist a 2-inch strip of lemon peel to release oils and drop into coffee. Serves one elegantly.

Cappuccino

Cappuccino is espresso plus milk that has been forced through a steaming attachment—an expensive item for a home kitchen—and it is served in a standard coffee cup, not a demitasse. You can whip very hot milk in a blender to achieve the frothy effect if you just can't wait until your favorite café opens.

> 1½ cups espresso
> 1½ cups hot, whipped milk
> ½ cup whipped cream
> ⅛ teaspoon nutmeg

Into four coffee cups, pour equal amounts of the espresso and milk. Float a dollop of whipped cream on each cup and sprinkle with nutmeg. Serves 4.

Cioccolino

Serve cappuccino in a soda glass and shave chocolate over the whipped cream. Omit the nutmeg.

Coffee Granità

A quick summer refresher, good at midday or as a dessert.

2 cups espresso
⅛ cup sugar
1 cup shaved ice
Whipped cream

Add sugar to espresso in the pot and let cool to room temperature. Place the shaved ice in a bowl and pour sweetened espresso over. Place mixture in freezer and stir once every hour until the mixture has the consistency of a slush cone. Place the mixture into small cups (fruit cups or punch cups are about right) and serve with a dollop of sweetened whipped cream on top of each. Serves 6.

Mocha Milkshake

¾ cup espresso, cooled to refrigerator temperature
¼ cup superfine sugar
¼ cup chocolate syrup
2 cups coffee ice cream
⅛ teaspoon cinnamon

Place all ingredients in blender and whip until frothy. Serve in tall glasses with a dusting of cinnamon. Makes 2.

Coffee Royale

For leave-taking. My grandfather used to serve this as the last offering of the day when we had special company.

Around twilight on reunion day we speak a bit about Grandma and Grandpa, each of us chiming in with our own best-remembered story, the intervals between the stories gradually growing longer. The bottle of anisette and the shot glasses for Coffee Royale appear along with the last pots of coffee.

We all take in the sunset, feeling the change to cooler, sweeter, dusky air. The chatter has subsided. We are aware of ourselves as a group, of all the members present and not present, of all the times we have sat this way, together. A few seconds of quiet, the familiar sort of quiet that comes from being with those you know best in the world and having shared everything of importance, then there is a sense of satisfaction with the day, a moment when the mood changes to *Basta!* Enough.

Finally, without ceremony, people start to pack up—deck chairs, picnic baskets, kids' shoes, serving plates, backs of envelopes with a niece's new address scribbled on them. Car doors slam. Horns toot. Good-byes are shouted all the way to the corner.

The reunion committee for next year picks up the black leatherette case containing everybody's addresses and the reunion history back to the beginning—and already the talk turns to next year. Next year at the reunion.

    1 cup strong, Italian black coffee
    1 ounce anisette (1 full shot glass)

Serve the coffee in its own cup and the anisette in its own shot glass. Each individual pours in his own anisette. Do not add milk or sugar.

Serves one unforgettably.

Bringing up a bottle of
Grandpa's Wine

DIRECTORY

FROM ITALY TO YOU:

Importers of Italian Foodstuffs and Kitchenware

These firms import a wide variety of foods, utensils, and kitchen machines from Italy and distribute them to retail outlets in North America. Contact them by mail or telephone to locate a store near you that handles items imported from Italy. Some importers also operate retail establishments, restaurants, delicatessens, and mail-order departments. These are noted in their listing. Information is summarized from *U.S.–Italy Trade Directory* (13th edition, 1979–80. New York: Italy–American Chamber of Commerce) and *Thomas Grocery Register 1980* (Vol. 2. New York: Thomas Publishing Co.). The names of other importers may be found in the yellow pages of your telephone directory.

ARIZONA
Phoenix:
Niccoli's Italian Grocer, Inc.
629 West Pierson
Phoenix, AZ 85013
(602) 266–9003

CALIFORNIA
Burlingame:
Tosi Trading Company
1499 Bayshore Hwy.
Burlingame, CA 94010
(415) 697–7960

Los Angeles:
D. DeFranco and Sons
1000 Lawrence St.
Los Angeles, CA 90021
(213) 627–8575

Pasquini Imports
1106 South Hope
Los Angeles, CA 90015
(213) 748–4952

Valley Cheese Company
4864 Valley Blvd.
Los Angeles, CA 90032
(213) 222–0879

Monterey Park:
Los Angeles Importing Co.
1160 Monterey Pass Road
Monterey Park, CA 91754
(213) 269–7221

San Bruno:
A. L. Desmond and Assoc.
P.O. Box 621
San Bruno, CA 94066
(415) 583–3316

San Francisco:
Sonoma Mission Foods
465 Cabot Rd.
San Francisco, CA 94111
(415) 761–4790

San Leandro:
Scandia Finer Foods Co., Inc.
1132 Beecher St.
San Leandro, CA 94577
(415) 632–1742

San Jose:
Bernard Food Industries, Inc.
222 S. 24th St.
San Jose, CA 95103
(408) 292–9067

South San Francisco:
Gourmet Specialties
228 Shaw Rd.
South San Francisco, CA
  94080
(415) 583–5900

Sunnyvale:
A. Giurlani and Brother, Inc.
1266 Kifer Rd.
Sunnyvale, CA 94086
(408) 738–0220

Sun Valley:
A.B.C., Inc.
9063 San Fernando Rd.
Sun Valley, CA 91352
(213) 769–6300

DISTRICT OF COLUMBIA
Washington:
Lencor, Inc.
1330 Wisconsin Ave. N.W.
Washington, DC 20007
(202) 338–2366

FLORIDA
Fort Lauderdale:
Montesco Brands, Inc.
2715 E. Oakland Park Blvd.
Fort Lauderdale, FL 33311
(305) 566–7399

Miramar:
Buitoni Foods Corp.
6151 Miramar Parkway
Miramar, FL 33023
(305) 625–5210

Sarasota:
V. M. Calderon, Inc.
P.O. Box 4241
Sarasota, FL 33578
(813) 366–3708

Tampa:
United Food Brokers, Inc.
110 W. Columbus Dr.
Tampa, FL 33614
(813) 229–0236

Vigo Importing Co.
4701 W. Comanche Ave.
Tampa, FL 33614
(813) 884–3491

ILLINOIS
Chicago:
Joseph Antognoli and Co.
310 W. Superior St.
Chicago, IL 60610
(312) 787–7990

Conte di Savoia
555 W. Roosevelt Rd.
Chicago, IL 60607
(312) 666–3471

Springfield:
Italian–American Importing
Co.
1000 E. Washington
Springfield, IL 62703
(217) 523–2321

KENTUCKY
Louisville:
John A. Conti Co.
4023 Bardstown Rd.
Louisville, KY 40218
(502) 499–8600

MARYLAND
Baltimore:
Joseph G. Vaccarino
224–230 S. High St.
Baltimore, MD 21202
(301) 752–2388
Also: Sole D'Italia wholesale
grocery.

MASSACHUSETTS
Boston:
A and J Distributors
236 Hanover St.
Boston, MA 02113
(617) 523–8490

Cambridge:
Cardello's, Inc.
6 Brattle St.
Cambridge, MA 02138
(617) 491–8888

Somerville:
Louis Metafora Co., Inc.
18 Kent St.
Somerville, MA 02143
(617) 625–5965

MICHIGAN
Royal Oak:
Lombardi Food Co.
605 E. Ten Mile Rd.
Royal Oak, MI 48067
(313) 548–4222

MINNESOTA
St. Paul:
Gourmet Foods, Inc.
860 Vandalia St.
St. Paul, MN 55114
(612) 646–2981

NEW JERSEY
Carlstadt:
Ramsey Imports
66 Broad St.
Carlstadt, NJ 07072
(201) 935–4500

Fort Lee:
New Horizon Trading Ltd.
1562 Lemoine Ave.
Fort Lee, NJ 07024
(201) 224–6022

Little Ferry:
Perugina Chocolate and
  Confections, Inc.
21 Main St.
Little Ferry, NJ 07643
(201) 641–3770

Rochelle Park:
Progresso Quality Foods
365 W. Passaic St.
Rochelle Park, NJ 07662
(201) 368–9459

NEW YORK
Bronx:
Domenico D'Angiola, Inc.
344 Hunts Point Terminal
  Market
Bronx, NY 10474
(212) 893–3060

Brooklyn:
R. DeMaio
2214 82nd St.
Brooklyn, NY 11214
(212) 783–1005

Gordon Products Co.
885 Flatbush Ave.
Brooklyn, NY 11226
(212) IN 9–0156

Moka D'Oro Coffee, Inc.
845 Grand St.
Brooklyn, NY 11211
(212) 387–2373

G. Nardella and Sons
25–27 Brooklyn Terminal
  Market
Brooklyn, NY 11236
(212) CL 1–7144

Paradise Products Corp.
59 Pearl St.
Brooklyn, NY 11201
(212) 855–1312

S. Scozzaro and Sons, Inc.
40 Brooklyn Terminal Market
Brooklyn, NY 11236
(212) CL 1–4661

Buffalo:
J. G. Pieri Co., Inc.
601 Bailey Ave.
Buffalo, NY 14206
(716) 825–5000

Corona (Queens):
Indelicato Food Distribution,
Inc.
107–05 51st Ave.
Corona, NY 11368
(212) 592–5800

Great Neck (Long Island):
Neil Esposito Associates
235 Clent Rd.
Great Neck, NY 11021
(516) 466–3335

Mineola (Long Island):
L. Della Cella Co., Inc.
100 E. Old Country Rd.
Mineola, NY 11501
(516) 742–5400

New York City (Manhattan):
Ferrara Foods and
Confections, Inc.
195 Grand St.
New York, NY 10013
(212) CA 6–6150
Also: restaurant and by mail.
Catalog.

Ferrero U.S.A., Inc.
489 Fifth Avenue
New York, NY 10017
(212) 687–6771

D. Lampariello and Son, Inc.
212 Grand St.
New York, NY 10013
(212) 226–3441

Manganaro's
488 Ninth Avenue
New York, NY 10018
(212) LO 3–5331
Also: restaurant, delicatessen,
take-out, phone order,
home delivery, and by
mail. Catalog.

Pozzi–Ginori Corp. of America
711 Fifth Avenue
New York, NY 10022
(212) PL 2–8790
Also: retail store.

Paprikas Weiss Importer
1546 Second Ave.
New York, NY 10028
(212) 288–6117
Also: retail store.

Niagara Falls:
Latina-Niagara Importing Co.,
Inc.
149 12th St.
Niagara Falls, NY 14303
(716) 284–0537

Schenectady:
  Oscusi Wholesale Grocery,
    Inc.
  819 Kings Rd.
  Schenectady, NY 12303
  (518) 377–8814

Woodside (Queens):
  Amer-Ital Foods, Ltd.
  34–56 58th St.
  Woodside, NY 11377
  (212) 779–2700

Yonkers:
  Nasco Industries, Inc.
  940 Nepperhan Ave.
  Yonkers, NY 10703
  (914) 423–2957

OHIO
Cleveland:
  Gust. Galluci Co.
  505 Woodland Ave.
  Cleveland, OH 44115
  (216) 241–5324

OKLAHOMA
Tulsa:
  International Trading
    Company of Tulsa
  10724 E. 55th Place South
  Tulsa, OK 74145
  (918) 628–1733

OREGON
Portland:
  Jacob Hamburger Co., Inc.
  5300 N. Channel Ave.
  Portland, OR 97217
  (503) 285–4531

PENNSYLVANIA
Hazleton:
  Hazleton Macaroni Co.
  221 E. Noble
  Hazleton, PA 18201
  (717) 454–0401

  John Roman
  531 W. First St.
  Hazleton, PA 18201

Philadelphia:
  Rosa Food Products Co., Inc.
  1312–1322 Federal St.
  Philadelphia, PA 19147
  (215) 467–2214

Pittsburgh:
  Pennsylvania Macaroni Co.,
    Inc.
  2010 Penn Ave.
  Pittsburgh, PA 15222
  (412) 471–9330

TEXAS
Dallas:
  Neiman-Marcus Company
  Main at Ervay Sts.
  Dallas, TX 75201
  (214) 741–6911
  Also: retail store and by mail.
    Catalog.

  Spaghetti Importing and
    Warehouse Co.
  1815 N. Market St.
  Dallas, TX 75202
  (214) 651–8475

VIRGINIA
Norfolk:
Fancy Foods of Virginia, Inc.
731–743 E. 25th St.
Norfolk, VA 23504
(804) 627–9568

WASHINGTON
Seattle:
Merlino Fine Foods
2822 Rainier Ave. South
Seattle, WA 98144
(206) 723–4700

The Napoleon Co.
1510 Norton Bldg.
Seattle, WA 98104
(206) 622–0720

WISCONSIN
Milwaukee:
Zurcoff Corporation
4465 N. Oakland Ave.
Milwaukee, WI 53211
(414) 962–4460

Plymouth:
Sargento Cheese Co., Inc.
P.O. Box 360
Plymouth, WI 53073
(414) 893–8484

CANADA
Vancouver:
Tosi Imported Food Co.
624 Main St.
Vancouver, BC V6A2V3
(604) 681–5740

PUERTO RICO
San Juan:
S. E. Albanese Svcs., Inc.
Fortaleza #311
San Juan, PR 00902
(809) 722–1261

INDEX

veal
  Parmesan, 116
  roast, stuffed, 114
  scaloppine, 115
vegetables, 75–101
  mixed raw, for antipasto, 38
  mixed summer, 81
  See also names

weddings
  cheesecake, 182
  dessert tray, 192
  rum cake Florentine, 184–91
white sauces, 52–53

zucchini bread, 99